F. J. A. Hort

F. J. A. Hort

Eminent Victorian

Graham A. Patrick

Biblical Studies: Historic Texts
BLOOMSBURY ACADEMIC COLLECTIONS

Bloomsbury Academic
An imprint of Bloomsbury Publishing Plc

B L O O M S B U R Y
LONDON · NEW DELHI · NEW YORK · SYDNEY

Bloomsbury Academic
An imprint of Bloomsbury Publishing Plc

50 Bedford Square
London
WC1B 3DP
UK

1385 Broadway
New York
NY 10018
USA

www.bloomsbury.com

BLOOMSBURY and the Diana logo are trademarks of Bloomsbury Publishing Plc

First published in 1987 by Sheffield Academic Press
This edition published by Bloomsbury Academic 2015

British Library Cataloguing-in-Publication Data
A catalogue record for this book is available from the British Library.

ISBN: HB: 978-1-4742-3164-0
       ePDF: 978-1-4742-3165-7
       Set: 978-1-4742-2900-5

Library of Congress Cataloging-in-Publication Data
A catalog record for this book is available from the Library of Congress

Series: Bloomsbury Academic Collections, ISSN 2051-0012

Printed and bound in Great Britain

HISTORIC TEXTS AND INTERPRETERS
IN BIBLICAL SCHOLARSHIP

General Editor:
Professor J.W. Rogerson (Sheffield)

Consultant Editors:
Professor C.K. Barrett (Durham)
Professor R. Smend (Göttingen)
Professor D.M. Gunn (Decatur)
Professor Pamela J. Milne (Windsor)

F.J.A. Hort. From a photograph in the possession of the author, presented by the late Professor Gordon Rupp.

F. J. A. HORT

EMINENT VICTORIAN

Graham A. Patrick

The Almond Press · 1988

To Margaret, Helen and Jeremy
with love and gratitude

Copyright © 1987 Sheffield Academic Press

Published by Almond Press
Editorial direction: David M. Gunn
Columbia Theological Seminary
Decatur, GA 30031-0520, U.S.A.
Almond Press is an imprint of
Sheffield Academic Press Ltd
The University of Sheffield
343 Fulwood Road
Sheffield S10 3BP
England

Typeset by Sheffield Academic Press
and
printed in Great Britain
by Dotesios (Printers) Ltd
Bradford-on-Avon, Wiltshire

British Library Cataloguing in Publication Data

Patrick, Graham A.
    F.J.A. Hort—eminent Victorian.—
    (Historic texts and interpreters in
    Biblical scholarship, ISSN 0263-119; 6).
    1. Hort, F.J.A.   2. Church of England—
    Clergy—Biography   3. Biblical scholars
    —Great Britain—Biography
    I. Title   II. Series
    230'.092'4   BX5199.H85

ISBN 1-85075-098-X
ISBN 1-85075-097-1 Pbk

CONTENTS

ACKNOWLEDGMENTS

For a Methodist to write the first study of a great nineteenth-century Anglican is not so surprising today as it would have been fifty years ago. The ecumenical climate in which we live affects the world of scholarship as well as the wider life of the churches, and this is something to be profoundly grateful for.

Among the many people who have helped me in this work, I must mention the Rev. Dr Leslie Mitton of Birmingham, who first introduced me to Hort's writings, and to whose teaching and encouragement I owe a lifelong debt; the late Professor Gordon Rupp of Cambridge, who gave me the portrait of Hort which is reproduced here; the late Dr Marcus Ward; and the Rev. Dr Cyril Rodd, whose unfailing interest has been a constant inspiration. Finally, I should like to thank my mother-in-law, Mrs Ann Parkin, for her help with typing; and Mr Dennis Doncaster for help with photography.

ABBREVIATIONS

Works by Hort

AJ	*The Apocalypse of St. John I-III*
ANF	*The Ante Nicene Fathers*
CE	*The Christian Ecclesia*
CS	*Cambridge and Other Sermons*
EJ	*The Epistle of St. James I^1-IV^7*
JC	*Judaistic Christianity*
PRE	*Prolegomena to St. Paul's Epistles to the Romans and the Ephesians*
TD	*Two Dissertations*
VS	*Village Sermons*
VSO	*Village Sermons in Outline*
WH	*The New Testament in the Original Greek*, Vol. II *Introduction and Appendix* (with B.F. Westcott)
WTL	The Way the Truth the Life

Other abbreviations

LL I/II	*Life and Letters of Fenton John Anthony Hort*, by Arthur Fenton Hort (2 vols.)
CUL	Cambridge University Library

INTRODUCTION

Reputation rises and falls with the years.

In 1897 William Sanday, Lady Margaret Professor of Divinity in the University of Oxford and one of England's leading biblical scholars, wrote a review article of Hort's *Life and Letters*.[1] He claimed that Hort was the greatest English theologian of the nineteenth century—superior even to Coleridge, Maurice and Newman in the power, originality, and depth of his thought.

Hort had died in 1892. His reputation then stood high amongst students and scholars at home and abroad, even though he had published only two books in his lifetime. Now, within the space of five years, he was being compared favourably with some of the greatest names of the century.

It was perhaps inevitable that such claims would not stand the test of time. Today the man so deeply admired, and even venerated, in the last decades of the Victorian era is virtually forgotten, certainly as a theologian. Biblical scholars know of him as a textual critic who, with Westcott, did some important pioneer work on the New Testament text. They may also know that he was a member of the Cambridge Triumvirate of Westcott, Lightfoot and Hort which played an important part in assisting the Victorian church to come to terms with biblical and historical criticism. In either case his name is linked with that of others, and little is known of him apart from this. It is rare to meet scholars who have a wider appreciation of his work.[2]

The striking disparity between the esteem in which Hort was held by his contemporaries and the low ebb of his reputation today makes a study of his life and work an urgent matter.

Renewed interest in the Victorian church makes it all the more necessary. Recent years have seen a spate of primary and secondary works on the period, and we are in a position now to see it in a much better perspective than our predecessors in the 1920s and 1930s, when there was such a strong reaction against Victorianism. We now know that the nineteenth century was the 'seed-bed' of many of our twentieth-century problems. Even so, there are still many gaps to be filled in our knowledge of that period. If Hort was indeed one of the foremost minds of the Victorian church, as many contemporaries thought, we need a study of his life and work.

Our aim is to give an account of his work and achievement against the background of his life. We shall then be in a position to assess both the exaggerated claims of some of his contemporaries and the myopia of our own times, which sees Hort as primarily a textual critic. In particular, it will emerge that Hort's personal contribution to some of the central biblical and theological issues of the later nineteenth century deserves to be taken very seriously.[3]

It must be said that Hort's reticence makes such a study peculiarly difficult. All through his life he was planning vast literary projects which were never realized. Ironically, almost the only project he ever completed was the New Testament text, with Westcott, which gives a quite misleading view of his priorities and interests. The main problem was his perfectionism which prevented him from publishing unless all the facts were available.

Fortunately, he was far more fluent in letters than in work prepared for publication, and we have felt the need to supplement his posthumously published fragmentary lectures with published and unpublished letters. We have also taken seriously his sermons as sources for his theology, and have discovered a volume of sermons, *Village Sermons in Outline* (1900), which does not appear to have been used previously as a primary source.

The primary source for biographical details is the two-volume *Life and Letters* by Hort's son which inspired Sanday's fulsome tribute, and which the late John Robinson said should be made compulsory reading for every intelligent ordinand![4]

Chapter 1

EARLY LIFE AND INFLUENCES

Fenton John Anthony Hort was born in Dublin on April 23rd 1828.
His father, Fenton Hort, came from a well-known Irish aristocratic
Protestant family. Cambridge-educated with private means, he had
no profession but was very active in public affairs and charitable
work. His mother, Anne Collett, the daughter of a Suffolk clergyman,
was well-educated, gifted and intelligent. She was a very strong
supporter of the Evangelical movement of the time and her views
were a dominant factor in the upbringing of her four children, of
whom Fenton was the eldest. The children were taught a close
knowledge of the Bible and a simple piety, and there was an
insistence on high moral standards. When Fenton later moved away
from the Evangelical views of his upbringing, there developed a
barrier between mother and son.

In 1837 the family moved to Cheltenham, at that time a centre of
the Evangelical movement. After attending a Preparatory school in
Laleham for two years, Fenton was sent in 1841, at the age of 13, to
Rugby School. Here he spent his formative years from thirteen to
eighteen, and on his own admission the school exercised a lasting
impression on him. The main influence was Thomas Arnold, who
had been headmaster since 1827. He died in 1842, but however brief
his personal contact the great man clearly made a deep impression on
the young Hort. We find him five years later marking the anniversary
of Arnold's death in his diary with red ink. In Arnold and the whole
ethos of Rugby he encountered a liberal influence in every way very
different from that of his upbringing.

In later years he acknowledged his debt to his former headmaster
in two directions. He believed that Arnold had helped him to see the
importance of politics.[1] He also ascribed his general theological
position, with his lifelong independence of all the main 'schools' and

parties, and yet many sympathies with the Broad Churchmen, to the influence of Arnold and Rugby. He wrote in 1865: 'What I am chiefly is no doubt what Rugby and Arnold made me . . . I have perhaps more in common with the Liberal party than with the others, through a certain amount of agreement in belief, and because in these days of suspicion and doubt I look upon freedom and a wide toleration as indispensable for the wellbeing of the Church' (LL II p. 63).

Another lasting influence upon the young man was the teaching of Bonamy Price, form-master of the 'Twenty'[2] at Rugby from 1836-50. Hort was later to dedicate his fragmentary commentary on 1 Peter[3] to Price, and it is clear that under his teaching the seeds were sown of Hort's later understanding of, and love for, language. His son quotes him as saying, in 1871, 'To him I owe all scholarship and New Testament criticism' (LL I p. 28) and singles out a 'belief in the trustworthiness of language' (LL II p. 54) as one feature of his later exegetical method which he learned from Price.

Hort was a promising pupil intellectually, nearly always at the top of his form. Even as early as this he displayed an exceptional breadth and thoroughness of knowledge, which were later to be characteristic of the mature man. Contemporaries remembered him as a rather awkward figure, not good at games, with a resolute, earnest face, blue eyes, bushy eyebrows and black straight hair.

By his last year at Rugby he had chosen the church as his profession. Letters from this period show that he is still very much the son of an Evangelical mother, but his choice of the church at this early stage must also have been affected by the influence of Arnold and his successor, A.C. Tait, later to become Archbishop of Canterbury.

In 1846 Hort went up to Trinity College, Cambridge, where he read for the Classics and Mathematics Tripos. Cambridge in the mid-1840s was a centre of lively debate over religious and social questions. The Evangelical wing of the Church of England had long been strong there, with Charles Simeon exercising a wide influence for almost half a century. Now, however, with Tractarianism developing in Oxford, there was suddenly a rival theological outlook, challenging Evangelicalism's ascendancy. Social questions were also 'in the air' for this was the period when the decline of the old privileged order was well under way, and the middle classes were increasingly aware of the gulf between themselves and the working classes—the period of Chartism.

This was a stimulating environment for the young man from Rugby, and he soon threw himself wholeheartedly into these controversies. At first he was happy with the Evangelical teaching of Dr Carus, one of Simeon's successors, but his letters show an increasing tendency to question it, especially its attitude to the sacraments and biblical criticism. By June 1848 he is quite critical of the whole Evangelical outlook, and there is clearly some tension with his parents over this. The liberal air he breathed at Rugby is now reinforced by other influences, which carry him in a very different direction from that of his home and childhood. To these influences we shall turn shortly.

It is important to note at this point the wide circle of friends Hort enjoyed from the beginning of his time in Cambridge. The fact that these were men of very varied interests involved in very different disciplines is a significant comment on his wide interests at this time. Among his earliest friends was John Ellerton, the Christian Socialist and hymn-writer. The two men found a common bond in the writings of F.D. Maurice, and became lifelong friends. Hort frequently poured out his heart to Ellerton and many of their letters have survived. Another friend was C.C. Babington, later to become Professor of Botany, with whom Hort shared an enthusiasm for botany. The two went on outings and holidays together, and Babington later would ask Hort to review very specialized books on the subject in the *Annals of Botany*. In April 1849 he wrote to Ellerton of his love for botany: 'I find it very advantageous and refreshing to be able to take refuge for a while from the circle of restless human interests of all kinds in something lower and yet with all the impress of perfection of its own kind,—something not spiritual, and yet rewarding research with views of infinite order and beauty' (LL I p. 100). Amongst other friends may be mentioned Daniel Macmillan, the publisher, with whom he was to be involved in more than one project; Henry Bradshaw, later to become Librarian of the University, another lifelong friend; and Clerk Maxwell, a brilliant scientist who was eventually to become Professor of Atomic Physics in the University.

Hort was to remain all his life a man of unusually wide interests, and that trait is observable in the young undergraduate with a wide circle of friends. Although he is reading Classics and Mathematics, he is passionately interested in philosophy, politics, natural science, and, of course, theology.

We have not mentioned the most significant of all his friendships which dates from this period. It is in these early years at Cambridge that Hort first meets Brooke Fosse Westcott and Joseph Barber Lightfoot, whose friendship and collaboration are to profoundly affect his whole life and work. Westcott became his classical 'coach' in January 1850, and they were together in Cambridge for another two years before Westcott went to Harrow School as a Master. By then they were already firm friends and had discovered a common interest in the problems of the Greek text of the New Testament, which was later to develop into a monumental project to revise the text. They now became regular correspondents. For almost half a century, Westcott was the closest of all Hort's friends. Lightfoot was elected to a fellowship at Trinity in 1852 with Hort and would later be his climbing companion on holidays in Switzerland and France. The three men were to work together on various projects, as we shall see, but Lightfoot was never so close to Hort at a personal level as was Westcott.

The three men are often described as the 'Cambridge Triumvirate', and it is assumed that because they worked together in a common cause they shared a common outlook on everything. This is far from the truth. There was obviously a good deal of common ground between them in biblical and theological matters, but quite profound differences existed also, and we shall frequently note the tensions which existed between the three.

We turn now to consider some of the principal influences on Hort at this crucial stage in his theological development, factors which reinforce the reaction against his Evangelical upbringing which began at Rugby and continued at Cambridge.

There was, first, the writings of Samuel Taylor Coleridge. It seems that Hort began to read Coleridge while at Rugby. This interest deepened while he was an undergraduate. Thus, in 1847, he records in his diary the dates of Coleridge's birth and death. The fruit of his deep and careful study of his works was the important and influential 'Essay on S.T. Coleridge' of 1856,[4] which shows a deep appreciation of Coleridge's mind. In 1857 he visited Ottery St Mary, Coleridge's birthplace. We may guess that Hort remained a lifelong admirer of the poet for as late as 1886 we see him describing Coleridge's *Aids to Confession* as 'a book to be read again and again' (LL II p. 329).

John Tulloch wrote of Coleridge that 'the later streams of religious thought in England are all more or less coloured by his influence'.[5] Hort was one of many Victorian thinkers who were conscious of their debt to him. He believed that he owed to Coleridge what we may almost call his 'intellectual awakening'. In a letter to F.D. Maurice in 1849, Hort described Coleridge as the one 'who first taught me to love light and to seek after truth, believing that it is God's will that we should attain them, and that He himself will guide us into them. . . ' (LL I p. 120). We shall also see, when we discuss the 1856 'Essay' on Coleridge, that the latter profoundly influenced Hort's whole theological outlook.

Second, and more important, were the writings and later the friendship of F.D. Maurice. Hort's relationship with Maurice has never been closely examined, and so it has not been appreciated how deeply Hort was influenced by Maurice at many levels. Of the Cambridge trio, Westcott has usually been regarded as the one who continued the Maurician tradition. But Hastings Rashdall was right to affirm that Westcott was 'never so consciously under the influence of Maurice as was his friend Dr. Hort'.[6] Although Hort never regarded himself as a 'disciple' of Maurice, there is no question that he stood firmly within the Maurician tradition, and that his theological outlook was profoundly influenced by Maurice's teaching and friendship.

His first contact with Maurice was through the latter's books which he began to read during his second year at Cambridge. In 1848 he read the *Kingdom of Christ* (1st edn, 1838), which made a deep impression on him, and the *Lord's Prayer* (1st edn, 1848), and in August of that year invented the Greek verb Μαυρικίζειν for one who is a disciple of Maurice. The following year there are more enthusiastic references in his letters to Maurice's understanding of the church and sacraments, and to his 'wonderful' *Prayer Book Sermons* (1st edn, 1849). By this time, Hort clearly felt such a degree of affinity with Maurice that in November 1849 he wrote a long letter to him, in which he set out his theological position, and especially poured out his heart to the older man on some of the issues on which he was perplexed and unhappy with contemporary theological orthodoxy. One of these issues was eternal punishment, and Hort's doubts about this are a remarkable anticipation of the views of Maurice himself, which were to lead to his expulsion from his chair at King's College, London in October, 1853 (see below, Chapter 2). He also consulted Maurice by letter for guidance for his reading in philosophy.

The first meeting with the man he had come to admire so deeply came in May 1850 in London, where he heard Maurice preach, and later had a meal at his home. Maurice's preaching made a profound impression on the young undergraduate. The following day Hort attended a Christian Socialist breakfast at which Maurice was present. From now on, a close friendship develops between the two men. Hort consulted Maurice before making important decisions, often read the proofs of his books before they were published, and stood firmly by him during the King's College affair in 1853. When Hort returned to Cambridge in 1872 after fifteen years in the parish, one of his greatest thrills was that he would now be a near neighbour of Maurice.

The hero-worship of the undergraduate, expressed particularly in his letters to John Ellerton, did not last. In time, Hort came to see some of Maurice's shortcomings, particularly his lack of interest in biblical criticism and the rise of science. He was well aware, however, how much he was indebted to Maurice. In a letter to Charles Kingsley in 1851 he referred to Maurice as he 'to whom we both, I believe, owe under God nearly all the better part of our being. . . ' (LL I p. 184). Twenty years later he was to say of Maurice's writings: 'To myself it seems that I owe to them chiefly a firm and full hold of the Christian faith. . . ' (LL II p. 155).

A comment by Hort's son on the reasons for his father's early attraction to Maurice is more precise. 'Here he found a religious teacher who seemed to bring the doctrines and sacraments of the Church into relation with the needs of individual and social life. In Maurice, moreover, there was not that distrust of the human reason which, so far as it characterised the "anti-Liberalism" of the Oxford Movement, made it impossible for Hort to be in complete sympathy with the leaders of that school' (LL I p. 61). To this we may add the appeal of Maurice's well-known concern to unite divergent theological views, and his studied independence of theological parties and schools. Hort was never himself to be closely associated with any of the main parties within the Church of England, and it is clear that he believed Maurice had influenced him in this respect.[7] We shall also see how deeply indebted to Maurice Hort was in his understanding of the sacraments and the atonement.

We have dwelt at some length on Hort's relationship with Maurice, partly because this has never really been elucidated. The facts suggest that Maurice was a dominant influence on the mind of the young Hort, and that in him we see a biblical scholar and theologian who was to perpetuate the distinctive Maurician theology and outlook.

Another early influence was the Oxford Movement, which was in its early stages when Hort was an undergraduate. He never read *Tracts for the Times* (1833-41) but we can detect the influence of Tractarianism in a letter of 1847, in which he enthuses about the church as 'the only center (sic) of all our hopes', that which alone can preserve us from the 'moral and intellectual seductions which swarm everywhere around' (LL I pp. 59-60). The following year he responds enthusiastically to the view that a 'High Church feeling' is gaining ground in Oxford and Cambridge (LL I p. 86). There is warm admiration for John Henry Newman—'him I all but worship' (LL I p. 231), he was to write in 1852—although later Hort offered some perceptive criticisms of the former Tractarian leader.

It is perhaps in his churchmanship that we may detect the permanent influence of the Movement. In these early years he developed a 'high' view of the church and ministry which he was to retain throughout his life. This must have owed something to the influence of this new movement in the Church of England. This is one respect in which Hort differed from Westcott and Lightfoot, neither of whom shared his High Church views. His agreement with High Churchmen was one of the reasons he gave for refusing to contribute to *Essays and Reviews* in 1858 (LL I p. 400). When he became a parish priest he introduced a High Church hymnbook into his churches. His son stresses his lifelong concern for liturgical detail and the aesthetic aspects of worship (LL I pp. 42-43).

It is possible, too, that Hort's vivid awareness of the corporate nature of the church and the Christian faith derived in part from the Oxford Movement. This, as we shall see later, was to become one of the central emphases in his theology. Something he said to his village congregation in 1867 expresses this concern well: 'Brethren, I am convinced that one reason why our lives so sadly need improvement is because we have so completely forgotten all about the Church' (CS p. 79). He made the same point two years later in a letter to John Ellerton: 'For a long time past I have been coming in various ways to feel that perhaps our most urgent need in the English Church is the creation of a true congregational life' (LL II p. 110). Here he is expressing a dissatisfaction with the excessive individualism of the Evangelical tradition in which he had been nurtured, having found in the New Testament, the writings of Maurice, and the Tractarians an altogether more satisfactory theology of the church.

Hort, however, never became closely associated with the Oxford Movement. For all its influence on his theology and churchmanship, he was deeply unhappy with one aspect of it—its intellectual cowardice. Many High Churchmen refused to face the challenge of the important critical and intellectual problems of the day. In 1854 he defined its main deficiency as 'the absolute ignoring of all the perplexing questions in theology and morals which are now being stirred,—in short, it is bread without yeast' (LL I p. 268). Eleven years later, in a perceptive and oft-quoted remark, he was to observe that for all their deep reading of the early Fathers, there was a total absence of any influence of the Greek Fathers on the leaders of the Oxford Movement (LL II p. 38). Hort saw in this neglect one of the reasons for the intellectual weakness of the movement. Whatever its good influence, it could not help people to face the challenge of biblical criticism and other problems which were crowding in upon the church at this time.

One other early influence on Hort which must be mentioned is that of Christian Socialism. The first phase of the movement, from 1848-54, has been well documented and the rôles of the leading figures closely studied. Hort was interested in their activities from the beginning. Thomas Arnold had inspired in him a deep interest in politics, and when he went up to Cambridge he seems to have been something of an 'angry young man', sympathetic to the Radical wing of contemporary politics, and very concerned about social and political issues. It is not surprising, therefore, that his first reactions to Christian Socialism are enthusiastic. He approves of its positive attitude toward Chartism (LL I p. 70), reads *Politics for the People*— the popular magazine of the movement—until it ceases publication in July 1848, and is thrilled by some of the contributions of Charles Kingsley and F.D. Maurice. Two years later he regretted this youthful enthusiasm: 'I am bound to confess that the 'Politics for the People' were too readily swallowed. I did not enough consider what I was about. . .' (LL I p. 133).

From 1850 onwards he is more critical of developments within the Christian Socialist camp. He has mixed feelings about the establishment of their co-operative workshops, and articulates his misgivings about their experiments in co-operation. He is not opposed to this in principle, but is unhappy about the attempt to make this principle into a system where 'the true individuality of each is lost, all that constitutes him a man, a moral being, is lost . . . ' (LL I p. 141). More important, such co-operative trading associations in no way challenged the basic selfishness of human nature, which was expressed very clearly in competition between industries. All they did was to substitute 'our interest' for 'my interest', and Hort could not see how anything was gained by that (LL I p. 141). There was substance to these criticisms. None of the co-operative associations lasted for very long, and later experiments developed with associations of consumers rather than producers.

Hort now decided that he must devote himself to a deep study of socialism, to examine the principles and deeper issues behind a movement such as Christian Socialism. It was already clear to him, however, that he could not be a Christian Socialist. He wrote a long letter (LL I pp. 132-45) to John Ellerton, himself a firm socialist, setting out his political and social views. The letter contains some trenchant criticisms of socialism in general and Christian Socialism in particular. Hort voices his misgivings about universal suffrage and co-operative ventures in industry, and his feeling that socialism was founded on selfishness.

It is soon after this, in May 1850, that he visited Maurice in London, and through him met some of the leading people in the movement—Ludlow, Vansittart Neal, Furnival, and Chevallier. He saw something of their activities, shared in a Bible Study with Maurice, Ludlow and Furnival, and had a conversation with Ludlow which greatly strengthened his feelings against socialism. All this only confirmed conclusions he had already drawn. He now very firmly repudiated the term 'Christian Socialist' as a description of his own position (LL I p. 163).

Such is a brief outline of Hort's 'flirtation' with Christian Socialism. For all his criticisms he remained a candid friend of the movement, and continued to read its literature. He was obviously aware of the significance of the events of those years, and indeed of the significance for Christianity of the spread of socialist ideas throughout Europe. In contrast, neither Lightfoot nor Westcott appears to have shown any interest in the 1848-54 movement.

Chapter 2

CAMBRIDGE

In 1850 Hort was placed third in order in the Classical Tripos, and in 1851 gained First Classes in both Moral and Natural Sciences. In 1852 he was elected to a fellowship at Trinity at the same time as J.B. Lightfoot.

The next five years were full and happy ones. Hort soon became deeply involved in the many-sided life of the University, and found the life of a Fellow congenial. It was an ideal opportunity for him to exercise his wide interests, and yet also a time when some future lines of study were emerging. It was a time of promise when the young Fellow of Trinity was beginning to make his mark in the University and in the world of scholarship.

In June 1851 Hort joined the famous 'Apostles' club, a secret debating society within the university. It is interesting that he consulted F.D. Maurice before joining. Through the 'Apostles' he came into contact with many distinguished men. He seems to have taken his membership seriously, often reading papers at its meetings, on a wide variety of subjects.

He became President of the Union in the October term 1852, a recognition of his frequent and impressive contributions to union debates between 1846 and 1852.

He was well-suited to the life of a College Fellow and had a strong conviction that this was his true vocation. There was opportunity and time for wide and thorough reading. He also enjoyed taking pupils. His letters from this period, with their comments on books and affairs of the time, display an amazing breadth of reading and maturity of judgment.

For all his wide interests, it is possible to detect two areas of study which are becoming of special concern to him. One is the New Testament, in particular its text and interpretation. A letter of

December 1851 shows him expressing his first interest in the Greek text of the New Testament and voicing his dissatisfaction with the so-called 'Textus Receptus'. Less than two years later, in a letter to John Ellerton, he writes these momentous words:

> He (i.e. Westcott) and I are going to edit a Greek text of the N.T. some two or three years hence, if possible... Our object is to supply clergymen generally, schools, etc., with a portable Gk. Test. which shall not be disfigured with Byzantine corruptions. But we *may* find the work too irksome (LL I p. 250).

The words are momentous because this was a project which was to engage the two men over the next twenty eight years. The end product was to be a magnificent and much-needed new critical edition of the Greek New Testament, but with Hort in particular it is undeniable that such a time-consuming project prevented him from pursuing other lines of study for which he was well equipped.

The other area which was increasingly becoming his special interest was Early Church History. His interest in this was stimulated by the vast amount of reading he did at this time for the Hulsean Prize Essay, the subject of which was 'Evidence of Christianity as exhibited in the writings of the early Apologists down to Augustine inclusively'. He did not win the prize, but here the foundations were laid for his lifelong interest in Church History. Later in 1852 he 'dreamed' of one day writing a massive history of the Ancient World from Abraham to the birth of Christ (LL I p. 234). His wry comment on this—'This is an alarming catalogue of labours, not a tenth part of which will, I suppose, ever be realised'—proved to be prophetic, for like many of Hort's 'dreams' it was never to be realized. Other interests and concerns were to prevent Hort from concentrating his time and energy upon Church History, but all his life he remained convinced of its importance and many of his writings reveal the historian's passion for detail and wide view.[1]

He became involved in numerous other academic projects during this period. A proposed Cambridge translation of the whole of Plato, which was never published, involved some years' work as one of the collaborators. His interest in Natural Science continued; he purchased a microscope in 1855 and in the same year examined for the Natural Science Tripos. His editing of Henry MacKenzie's Hulsean Essay on 'The Beneficial Influence of the Christian Clergy on European Progress in the First Ten Centuries' involved verifying thousands of references, and took up a whole year's work. He was also learning

Hebrew. According to Hort's son, it was at this time in his life, when he was becoming involved in more and more activities and academic projects, that he began the habit of sitting up far into the night to study, which was to have permanent effects on his health and which in later years he was to regret.

In 1853 F.D. Maurice was expelled from his chair at King's College, London for his unorthodox views on eternal punishment. Hort was indirectly involved in this controversy because of his friendship with Maurice, and in particular because of the letter he had written to Maurice four years earlier on this very issue. An examination of this letter, Maurice's reply, and Hort's reaction to the King's College affair will provide a very helpful insight into Hort's general theological position at this period in his life.

The belief in the eternal punishment of the wicked in hell was very widely accepted by Christians in the first half of the nineteenth century. It was held to have a firm biblical basis, and to be the chief sanction for morality. It was assumed that 'eternal' meant 'everlasting', and that 'punishment' meant dereliction and torment without end. Tender consciences and thoughtful people were aware of the difficulty of reconciling it with the love of God.[2] Like the substitutionary view of the atonement, however, it was regarded as part of the common currency of faith.

Hort was only twenty-one when he wrote to Maurice (LL I pp. 116-23) confessing his own very serious misgivings about eternal punishment. He admits that it is sanctioned by the Gospels and the Apocalypse, as well as by the church's liturgy and the Athanasian Creed. He can see also that it is a sanction for morality. Belief in punishment beyond the grave is a strong reason for men repenting of their evil even on their deathbed. He is nevertheless deeply unhappy about it. He can see no allusion to it, for instance, in the New Testament Epistles, whose whole tone is quite opposed to the idea. In particular he is haunted by St Paul's statement 'As in Adam all die, even so in Christ shall all be made alive'. Hort notes that 'the same universality is given to the one clause as to the other' (LL I p. 117).

He then mentions two common objections to the doctrine. He feels the force of the argument that it is impossible to draw a single line between men, so that the good go to heaven and the bad to hell, for the gradations between men are infinite: 'Every one is perpetually falling; the difference is but slight between him who falls at last utterly away, and him who just succeeds in not losing hold of his

Lord' (LL I p. 118). He can also see no answer to the Universalist objection to the doctrine, namely, 'that finite sins cannot deserve an infinite punishment' (*ibid.*). Hort confesses that the whole question of the existence of evil is focused for him in the doctrine of eternal punishment, and that so far he has not been able to reconcile the fact of God with the existence of evil in this form.

Another of his doubts centres on the question of Substituted Punishment. The most popular contemporary view of the atonement asserted that Christ suffered in our place. Hort cannot see how an acceptance of this can dispense with the need for our own suffering and punishment for our sins.

> The fact is, I *do not see how* God's justice can be satisfied without *every man's* suffering in his own person the full penalty for his sins. I *know* that it *can*, for if it could not in the case of some at least, the whole Bible would be a lie; but if in the case *of some*, why not *of all?*
> (LL I p.120)

Hort also mentions in passing another doubt he has about the doctrine—the inconsistency of the notion that God punishes sin by sin with the Christian belief that God cannot be the author of evil.

He concludes his letter by mentioning his emotional reaction to the doctrine of eternal punishment, the 'twinge of shrinking horrour' (sic) he feels when it is asserted (LL I p. 122). To him it is a paradox that it should be proclaimed as part of the 'good news' of Christianity.

Hort's long letter effectively gathers together most of the contemporary objections to the doctrine. It is also very revealing of his theological development in this period. It appears from this that the popular doctrine of eternal punishment is the focus of many of his difficulties with the traditional, evangelical version of Christianity with which he had been brought up. He had read enough of Maurice's works to know he was writing to one who would sympathize with his questioning. What he could not have foreseen was that it was precisely this issue which was to be the pretext for Maurice's expulsion from his chair at King's four years later.

The letter Maurice wrote in reply to Hort[3] was later to form the basis of his defence against his critics.[4] We can only briefly note its main contentions here. These centre on his interpretation of the word 'eternal' which he takes from John 17.3: 'This is eternal life, that they may know thee the only true God, and Jesus Christ whom thou hast sent'. Maurice argues that eternal life here cannot refer to the future. Our Lord intends us 'to see eternity as something altogether out of time, to connect it with Him who is, and was, and is to come'.[5] 'Eternal' in the New Testament is a quality of life, not an endless time. 'I cannot apply the idea of time to the word eternal', writes Maurice. Our Lord's conception of eternity is something quite different from the popular idea.

Maurice denied that this led to universalism. The righteousness of God condemns sin, and it is possible for men to persist in their sin and to resist the divine love. But we cannot set limits to what the love of God may achieve in this or any other life.

> I know that we may struggle with the Light, that we may choose death. But I know also that Love does overcome this rebellion. I know that I am bound to believe that its power is greater than every other.[6]

Maurice is conscious here that he has come very close to the universalist position. He is content, however, with re-stating the paradox inherent in his argument:

> I dare not fix any limits to the power of His love. I cannot tell what are the limits to the power of a rebel will . . . I am obliged to believe that we are living in a restored order; I am sure that restored order will be carried out by the full triumph of God's loving will. How that should take place while any rebellious will remains in His universe I cannot tell . . .[7]

Maurice clearly believed that impenitence at death does not necessarily imply the soul's damnation or consignment to everlasting torment.

Reading the letters of Hort and Maurice together, one cannot help contrasting the clarity of Hort's thinking with the vagueness and impreciseness of the man whom he had asked for advice. It is undeniable, too, that Hort was something of a catalyst in this whole affair, since the need to reply to his letter must have been one of the factors which led Maurice to openly challenge the traditional understanding of eternal punishment.

How did Hort react to the controversy that blew up in 1853? By this time he had become a friend of Maurice so he felt much personal distress at his plight. He writes of the 'sad event which is haunting my mind incessantly' (LL I p. 261). He was instrumental in circulating an address of sympathy for Maurice, which entailed a great deal of correspondence (LL I p. 242). He was also deeply disturbed because his own views on eternal punishment were substantially the same as Maurice's. The older man's letter had obviously entirely convinced Hort.

> I fully and unwaveringly agree with him in the three cardinal points of the controversy: (1) that eternity is independent of duration; (2) that the power of repentance is not limited to this life; (3) that it is not revealed whether or not all will ultimately repent (LL I p.275).

Reading and reflection had confirmed him in his support for the views of his friend, for he quotes Plato, St Augustine and Clement of Alexandria as authorities to whom one could appeal for support for such views (LL I pp. 261, 266, 269).

Hort therefore aligned himself totally with the view of Maurice in this controversy. He defended him publicly, as we have seen, and most vigorously in private correspondence. Later in life, Hort was to say that he had always felt himself to be something of a heretic in other men's eyes. Here, possibly, was his first awareness of swimming against the theological tide, finding himself sharing views which are pronouncedly heretical.

We have dwelt on this issue at some length because it is an important one for our understanding of Hort's early theological stance. It is also important in its own right for understanding the development of nineteenth-century theology. We need not agree with all that Maurice said—even his most sympathetic interpreters admit that his thinking about life and death was cast too much in Johannine the Platonist terms[8]—to recognize that he did a great service to theology by bringing the question of eternal punishment out into the open. In 1888 Benjamin Jowett looked back and saw that theology had progressed since the 1850s:

> Our problems are not so serious as those of thirty or forty years ago. Then men thought they had to receive as a revelation from God that which conflicted with their sense of justice, and puzzled themselves with trying to reconcile God's goodness with the doctrine of eternal punishment.[9]

As we have seen, Hort played no small part in this important controversy.

We have already noted that Hort had decided to enter the church during his last year at Rugby. By 1853 he was preparing for his ordination and he wrote to Samuel Wilberforce, Bishop of Oxford, asking to be ordained during Lent 1854. His ordination as deacon took place in St Peter's Oxford in April 1854, and he was ordained priest in Ely Cathedral in 1856.

Another interest in these years was the establishment of a Working Men's College in Cambridge. This was modelled on the famous London College, with which F.D. Maurice was closely connected, and opened in 1855. Hort was actively involved in its foundation. He spent much time on the work of the Council and did some lecturing there in these early years. He had high hopes that it would help to bridge the gap between the classes for it brought together working men and representatives of the University. He also felt it would have good effect on the University. In 1856 a similar College was founded in Oxford, and Hort went to Oxford for the first anniversary meeting.

In 1856 Hort contributed to a collection of *Cambridge Essays* an 'Essay on S.T. Coleridge'. It was the fruit of some ten years' reading of Coleridge, which, we noted, began while Hort was at Rugby. It must be regarded as one of the earliest attempts to interpret the thought of the poet-philosopher, and in the light of the immense interest in Coleridge as a philosopher-theologian in recent years there is a prophetic quality about it. Hort was one of the first people to see the significance of Coleridge for theology.

This long essay shows how deeply Hort had read in philosophy since going up to Cambridge. He is well acquainted with German thinking—Kant, Lessing, Herder, Fichte and Schleiermacher are all mentioned, and there is a fine analysis of the relation between Kant and Coleridge. He also quotes Greek and English philosophers widely. This philosophical grounding enabled Hort to see Coleridge in a broad European setting. It was also to give his own theology a distinctive character, and is one of the points where he had an advantage over Westcott and Lightfoot, neither of whom had read so deeply in this field.

In the essay Hort picks out certain characteristics of Coleridge's thought. He regards his love of freedom as his most characteristic emphasis. 'An unquenchable thirst for liberty is the one unchanging spring of his whole life. . . The impulse which came from politics spread through every region in which he ever cared to move' (p. 313). Freedom must 'be followed through errour (sic) and blindness as the last and most awful duty of man' (*ibid.*). And Hort makes it clear that this is an emphasis very much needed in his own time when there is a danger that freedom may become a 'thing suspect'. It is not clear precisely what he is referring to here. It is likely, however, that he has in mind freedom of enquiry in relation to the new biblical criticism, an issue which was to emerge very sharply in the later debate over *Essays and Reviews* (1st edn, 1859). Then, as now, Hort regarded it as vital that no restrictions should be placed upon scholars in their investigations.

Hort also draws attention to the polarity of Coleridge's thought, his awareness of the many-sidedness of truth.

> Classification is our pride and pleasure; and woe be to that which refuses to be classified. An author whose opinions will not range with those of any recognised party, or whose works never seem quite rightly lodged in any one division of a well-regulated library, occupies in general estimation what was once the place of a zoophyte or a platypus,—an uncanny creature, possibly of demoniacal origin.

Such a divine monster was Coleridge (p. 292). Coleridge's writings range over philosophy, theology and aesthetics and part of his appeal to Hort, as to other Victorians, was the possibility he offered of a unity between these different branches of knowledge.

Hort also expounds Coleridge's Platonism, his distinction between 'Reason' and 'Understanding', and his emphasis upon truth as something appropriated not by logical processes alone, but by the response of the whole person. In this respect he sees Coleridge as standing against the stream that flowed from the Enlightenment, with its great stress upon rationality, pointing his age in quite a different direction. We shall see that this aspect of Coleridge deeply affected Hort's whole theological outlook, most noticeably in his Hulsean lectures, *The Way the Truth the Life*.

It is surprising that there is no mention of Coleridge's *Confessions of an Inquiring Spirit* (1st edn, 1840), in which the latter set out his attitude to the inspiration of Scripture—a book describing a new approach to inspiration which was to have profound influence later in the century. Hort was to become very much involved in the debate about 'inspiration', and his views seem to be coloured by Coleridge's seminal work. There is, however, no reference to the *Confessions* in this essay.

The essay displays a remarkable breadth of knowledge and maturity of judgment for a young man of 28. It suggests that here was a philosophical theologian of great promise, one who had found in the writings of Coleridge many answers to his own deepest questions.

In February 1857 Hort became engaged to Fanny Holland, the daughter of a Lincolnshire family. It was impossible under the college statutes at that time to remain as a married don, and so Trinity College presented him with the living of St Ippolyts-cum-Great Wymondley near Hitchin, where the couple moved in June 1857 after their wedding.

Chapter 3

THE PARISH PRIEST

Hort spent the next fifteen years, from 1857 to 1872, in rural Hertfordshire. It was a significant period in his life. He still kept his links with Cambridge, but he had now left the academic seclusion of the University for the wider world and the life of an ordinary parish. In time he would long to be back in Cambridge, but it is undeniable that these years in a parish were valuable in many respects. They were years of controversy in the Church of England when first *Essays and Reviews* and then *Origin of Species* raised fundamental theological issues and led to fierce debates amongst educated Christians. We shall examine Hort's response to these controversies in the next chapter.

He preached his opening sermon in his parish on the words of Isaiah which Jesus chose to preface his own ministry.[1] The subject was 'What is the gospel?' Hort is quite emphatic that it is concerned with man's earthly and material life and not just his spiritual condition. 'Every attempt to raise men out of a condition of depression and suffering is a carrying out of God's gospel, and part of the work which He is ever accomplishing' (VS pp. 10-11). Here we are reminded of his interest in Christian Socialism. There are echoes, too, of Coleridge and Maurice when Hort describes the gospel as 'above all things a gospel of *freedom* and *light*' (VS pp. 12-13). The sermon ends with a firm declaration that the centre of the good news is the love of God:

> That God's mind towards man is from first to last love altogether without any reserve, and that His various dealings with man, whether of mercy or of judgment, are but the wise and orderly workings of His love, this is the gospel which we have received from Christ and His Church (VS p. 15).

This is a significant statement, the background to which is Hort's long wrestling with the doctrine of eternal punishment. It seems that he found it so unacceptable because, like Maurice, he could not reconcile it with his belief in the love of God, which was the beginning and end of the gospel.

We can only surmise as to the reaction of the congregation to their new parish priest. They would hardly have detected the echoes which we have heard behind Hort's words. But there is little doubt that there were emphases here which would have sounded strange to those fed on a simple evangelical diet. Here was someone painting on a broader canvas than they had been used to. Here was someone, too, who would make demands of his hearers, for this was a closely argued, theological sermon, simple but deep. It made few concessions to a village congregation.

Hort's new charge was a double parish. The vicarage was at St Ippolyts, which is about two miles from Hitchin. Each parish had a school and a Sunday school. He threw himself fully into the parish round of services, visiting, teaching in Sunday school and day school, and the wider involvements which came the way of a parish priest. He removed a barrel organ from one of his churches, and gave a great deal of attention to improving the services and the music. As we saw earlier, he introduced a new High Church hymnbook to improve the worship. There was no feeling, as some have suggested,[2] that he believed he was wasting his time in a country parish. Hort's son points out that his father never felt this, and later in life was distressed if anyone suggested it. He had been preparing for such work for some years, and in any case he loved country life, with its walks, gardening, and closeness to the natural world which he loved.

Nevertheless, as time passed the conviction grew on him that the life of a parish priest was not his true sphere of work. Arthur Hort says that he first voiced his doubts to Westcott as early as 1861 (LL I p. 358). Five years later he writes to a friend quite openly of his unfitness for the work:

> Owing to peculiarities of temperament partly but not wholly connected with health, I have never, to speak plainly, been able to adapt myself properly to parochial work. With the highest sense of its dignity and importance in itself . . . I have most unwillingly been compelled to doubt my own fitness for it (LL II pp. 74-75).

His greatest problem was his habitual shyness and reserve. This was less of a handicap for a Fellow in a Cambridge college, but for a parish priest it was a real drawback, making pastoral work particularly difficult. There was also the acute problem of self expression through sermons. Hort's son describes how he would regularly sit up well into the early hours of the morning to write sermons, a habit which would inevitably have an effect on his health sooner or later. We may note in passing that all his life Hort was to find it difficult to express himself in work prepared for publication or for public consumption. In contrast, his letters are fluent and models of lucidity. As well as being a perfectionist, Hort appears to have felt very strongly a heavy sense of responsibility where public utterance was concerned.

The initial outcome of all this was that he suffered a breakdown in health after just two years at St Ippolyts. For the next two years he had to take long summer holidays in the Alps. In 1862 a doctor advised him to give up parish work altogether for three years, and so he left his parish from 1863 to 1865, spending the winters at Cheltenham and the summers in the Alps.

This was more than a mere physical breakdown in health. It was rather what we today would describe as a 'nervous breakdown'. The growing conviction that he was unsuited to parish life together with his habit of always living and working at full stretch took their toll. The daily routine of parish life became unbearable. The academic work he was engaged in in his spare time was a therapy to him. There is a tell-tale sentence in a letter to Macmillan, the publisher, in January 1863, in which Hort begs for more time to finish some work for publication: 'If I had no parish and no nerves, it might be different' (LL I p. 472).

The three years away from the parish enabled him to devote more time to his interests in natural history. While at Cheltenham he spent two days a week in the Cotswolds collecting fossils and studying the local geology and botany. Westcott and Lightfoot were concerned about this, feeling that he was devoting more time to geology than to the various theological projects he was engaged in at the time. They really believed he was wasting his valuable time, and must have worried that their friend, who was so dissatisfied with much of the contemporary geological mapping of his area, would turn to this as an outlet for his immense enthusiasm.

The summers in the Alps enabled him to make a close study of the Alpine flora. He made rough lists of plants for the different valleys. His letters are full of comments on the local flora. He noted the local geology, too, and even met the distinguished geologist, Sir Charles Lyell, with whom he enjoyed 'a long geological talk' (LL II p. 41).

Sketching was another of his interests he was able to pursue during this period.

In 1865 he returned to St Ippolyts. It is significant that the following year he stood for the chair of Moral Philosophy at Cambridge. He was not elected—the successful candidate was his friend, F.D. Maurice—but the fact that he was a candidate shows that his mind had now turned increasingly towards Cambridge. His friends tried hard now to find him a university post. He himself felt that he was more suited to university work than the parish.

Here it is helpful to pause briefly to see how deeply Hort had become involved in numerous academic projects during these years in the parish. Although he believed that this was therapeutic in the midst of his parish routine, the cumulative effect of his wider and wider involvement must only have added to the pressures upon him.

The chief literary work of his parish years was the Greek text. Throughout the fifteen years he gave much of his spare time to it. Westcott would come down from Harrow in the school holidays and they would work together on it for four days at a time. Typical is this extract from a letter of January 1859: 'Westcott's four days dwindled, alas! to three, but we worked incessantly Wednesday, Thursday, and Friday. Alas! we only finished St.Matthew and three chapters of St.Mark' (LL I p. 402). Even during his convalescent years he found time and energy for this. Thus it was while he was in Switzerland in the summer of 1864 that he finished the first draft of the 'Introduction' to the Text. The winter of 1864–65 was a time of very concentrated work when he and Westcott began their final revision, which unfortunately was to take far longer than they anticipated.

This, then, was Hort's main academic work during his parish years, one which he believed must have priority because of its importance. For a time he made this the excuse for not becoming involved in other projects, but this resolve weakened, especially during his later years at St Ippolyts. One constraint was finance. The need to make ends meet led to his involvement, as early as 1859, in writing a life of Simon de Montfort for boys. The book did not materialize, only a learned article in *Macmillan's Magazine* for 1864, but Hort's typically thorough approach meant that a great deal of time was wasted on researching it. In 1860 Hort joined with Westcott and Lightfoot in a Commentary scheme for the whole of the New Testament. We shall discuss this important project, and its fruits, in a later chapter. For now we may note that the struggle to complete some preliminary essays on the letter of James was another pressure upon him. 'It haunts me perpetually, and yet I find it most hard to get anything on paper' (LL II p. 85), is his very characteristic comment to John Ellerton.

Another involvement was in a Dr Smith's *Dictionary of Christian Biography*. The invitation to participate in this came in 1868, and Hort was asked to contribute articles on the Gnostics and the Greek fathers who opposed them—Irenaeus, Hippolytus and Epiphanius. This, too, involved him in an immense amount of research, to the despair of Lightfoot and Westcott, who felt that this was yet another distraction from more important matters like the Greek Text and the Commentary scheme. Before long, Hort too regretted his participation in this particular project.

The same year, 1868, Hort was an Examiner in the Moral Science Tripos at Cambridge. Two years later he received an invitation to join the New Testament Revision Company. In 1871 he became Examining Chaplain to the Bishop of Ely and he delivered the Hulsean lectures at Cambridge. About all these things we shall have more to say later. Enough has been said to show that by his last years at St Ippolyts Hort had committed himself to a bewildering variety of academic projects. And it must be remembered that we have not mentioned at all his involvement in the debates surrounding *Essays and Reviews* and *Origin of Species*, nor the various books he dreamed of writing but which, typically, came to nothing; such as a Greek Grammar based on the New Testament, for which he did a good deal of work, and a history of the Ante-Nicene period ('one of my many castles in the air' [LL I p. 393]).

It must be said that there was a failure to concentrate interests in Hort which is seen most acutely during this period. He found it difficult to say no. It was partly that his interests were so wide, and he believed it was important that scholars should not specialize too narrowly. This was one of the reasons for his objection to the establishment of a Theological Tripos in Cambridge. But even allowing for this, it is difficult to deny that Hort spread his research far too widely and allowed himself to become involved in projects which were not really worthy of his time. Certainly, that was the feeling of his closest colleagues, Westcott and Lightfoot, who were often urging him to concentrate on the really important work.

In the light of all this, it is not surprising that Hort found the final years of parish work quite crushing in their wide range of responsibilities. 'It is work, work, work from breakfast to bed, and still always with the feeling that three-quarters are left undone, and that harm is constantly happening to others in consequence', he wrote to his sister in 1870. He goes on: 'As regards the parish I am always unhappy, always feeling how much is needed in this straggling place which is quite beyond me; the thought both frets me day and night as regards myself, and also suggests that some one else might have better success . . . ' (LL II p. 121). At the same time, according to his son, the struggle to make ends meet became more acute, adding extra pressure. It is not surprising that Hort always believed he had been a failure as a parish priest, and after he left St Ippolyts he would not revisit it for a number of years.

If we would understand something of Hort's theological position and development during his years in the parish we must turn to the letters written, and the sermons preached to his village congregation, during his time there.

An illuminating letter of 1865 throws light on his understanding of the nature of theology.

> Theology is now with me as it has always been, the chief subject of interest, while I have by no means abandoned the other subjects of various kinds which have occupied me at different times. To give them up would be not merely a severe privation to myself, but an injury to whatever little I may ever be able to do in Theology, for that is a study which always becomes corrupted by being pursued exclusively (LL II p. 63).

Hort's friends, as we have seen, were often pleading with him to narrow his interests and concentrate his energies. His refusal to do this was based upon a conviction about the very nature of theology.

In the same letter there is a comment on his theological position in relation to the 'parties' of the day. 'In Theology itself I am obliged to hold a peculiar position, belonging to no party, yet having important agreements and sympathies with all, and possessing valued friends in all' (*ibid.*).

As well as this sense of isolation, Hort seems to have felt increasingly aware of his theological unorthodoxy. This emerges particularly in correspondence in 1871 over the Bishop of Ely's invitation to Hort to become his Examining Chaplain. Hort has deep misgivings about accepting and one of the reasons is his feeling that he is not sufficiently orthodox to hold such a position. He writes to Westcott: 'Ought he (i.e. the Bishop) not for that special work to have some one who can naturally and truthfully move more near the beaten tracks?' (LL II p. 153). Hort then writes to the Bishop: 'My fear is that, partly in views, and still more in sympathies, I do not sufficiently conform to any of the recognised standards to be a fit person for the special post which you offer me' (LL II p. 155). He then goes on to mention areas where he is aware of being outside the mainstream—his difficulties over parts of the Old Testament, his interest in biblical criticism, natural science, and philosophy, and his strong feeling that they must be pursued without any reserve and regardless of conclusions reached. He also mentions, significantly, his friendship and affinity with F.D. Maurice. After a further exchange of correspondence concerning Hort's view of the doctrine of the atonement, the Bishop was happy to appoint Hort to the position. The letters between them, however, are most revealing of Hort's strong sense of being theologically unorthodox.

There is an unpublished letter of 1864 in which he expresses this feeling even more forcefully. The subject under discussion is the radical changes in form he and Westcott were thinking of introducing into their edition of the Greek Text of the New Testament. Westcott appears to have written to Hort suggesting that they would be branded as heretics for doing this. Hort replies: 'I can hardly remember when I have felt myself anything but a predestined heretic in the eyes of others'.[3] The context is the textual work the two friends were engaged upon, but it seems fair to take it as a more general comment about Hort's feeling of being viewed with suspicion by orthodox churchmen.

We have dwelt upon this particular aspect of Hort's self-awareness at this period of his life because it has not really been pointed out before. Hort, together with his two friends, has usually been regarded as a pillar of theological orthodoxy. Certainly, in later years Hort became a revered and widely respected figure in the Victorian church. But at this middle period of his life he is aware of being a rather suspect figure, too bold and open-minded for many of his contemporaries. Is this the reason why, unlike Westcott and Lightfoot, he was never to attain high ecclesiastical office?

It is pertinent to ask here to what extent his close association with F.D. Maurice was responsible for this reputation. We have seen how Hort's friendship with Maurice continued unabated after the King's College affair, and noted how Hort mentions defensively his affinity with Maurice in his correspondence with the Bishop of Ely. It is possible that this was a factor in the reputation he had gained.

If we look closely at some of the sermons Hort preached to his village congregation, we can see how deeply Maurice had influenced Hort. This is most apparent in his theology and understanding of baptism. Hort preached no fewer than six sermons on baptism between 1867 and 1871, and they reveal an understanding of the sacrament rather different from that current in Tractarian and Evangelical circles at the time.

Briefly, we may say that the Tractarians re-asserted strongly the Prayer Book doctrine of baptismal regeneration, while the Evangelicals understood baptism as simply admission into the church, conversion being the most important moment in the Christian life. There was uneasy tension between these two approaches, and at times open conflict, as in the celebrated Gorham case of 1847.[4]

Hort, who as we have seen had High Church sympathies, believed in baptismal regeneration, but unlike many Tractarians he refused to see baptism as an isolated act. He often stresses the importance of confirmation as a necessary sequel to baptism, and one of his sermons has the title 'Baptism and Confirmation' (CS pp. 83-97). Pusey had asserted: '"Regeneration" is the gift of God, bestowed by Him, in this life, in Baptism only'.[5] Hort is more aware of the continuities in the Christian life. 'Baptism is not a momentary thing, but the sign of a whole life's profession, always beginning, never ended' (VSO p. 105).

Where he departs most sharply from both Tractarian and Evangelical teaching is in his understanding of baptism as a declaratory act of God. He believed that the prime importance of this sacrament was in its declaration of what God has done. In baptism 'God declares us to be His children' (CS p. 89). The whole rite is a pledge of this. The Bible and Prayer Book make it quite clear that we are children of God. 'But He has further ordained a certain pledge by which each man may assure himself that he has a right to say , "I am a child of God"; and that pledge is baptism' (CS p. 90). Hort repudiates the belief that something almost magical takes place within a child at baptism. Rather, 'the whole baptism, water and words together, is what Christ Himself appointed as the way of entrance into the Kingdom of God. God by it formally acknowledges the child as His own, gives him by it a right and title to enter on all the benefits which belong to His children' (*ibid.*).

Understood in this way, baptism is primarily something that God does rather than anything we do. 'It is much more God's act than man's act. The child has to be brought to the church, and promises are made for him. But *the* thing is God blessing the child: all the doings of men—church, clergyman, sponsors, parents, child—are nothing beside that. God speaks, it is for men to hear' (VSO p. 89).

The other strong emphasis in Hort's understanding of baptism was its testimony to the corporateness of the Christian faith. Baptism was the entrance into the Christian church, the means by which a child was 'grafted into the body of Christ's Church' (CS p. 82). He was deeply unhappy with much contemporary practice, which regarded the sacrament as mainly an individual, hole-in-the-corner affair. He condemned the practice of conducting baptisms outside the context of public worship. It must be done in the presence of the whole congregation, for they participate in the act and receive the child in Christ's name. Baptism must be 'the act not of the clergyman only, but of the whole congregation or Church' (CS p. 86).

Here we touch upon one of the main themes of Hort's whole theology. He was deeply aware of the corporate nature of the Christian faith, the 'church' dimension. The individual character of so much of the church life of his time was a constant source of concern to him. His writings reveal a fervent desire to restore to the church of the nineteenth century that corporate dimension that was so apparent in the apostolic communities and the theology of St Paul, particularly in the letter to the Ephesians. Baptism was one of the most potent symbols of the sense of belonging to one another which should pervade the Christian community: 'Baptism is thus more striking than any sermon on the blessing we are meant to be to each other, and to the babe who is to grow up amongst us. All single separate dealings are set aside. As baptized, men are never strangers to a heavenly family . . . ' (VSO p. 105). 'No Christian child is a lonely creature . . . it shares, long before it knows, in all the life and doings of those around it' (VSO p. 94).

Here is an understanding of baptism quite different from that of most contemporary churchmen, yet remarkably similar to that of Maurice. We find in the latter's writings a strong assertion of the declaratory view of the sacrament, a continual awareness of its social significance, and a frequent stress on confirmation as a necessary sequel to it. It is arguable that it is at this point that Maurice's influence on Hort is most evident. Indeed, Alec Vidler makes the remarkable claim that Maurice's understanding of baptism is expressed most clearly and simply in one of Hort's sermons![6]

Another group of sermons, preached in 1868, throws light on Hort's attitude to the Bible. In a series of twelve sermons he works through the Old and New Testaments to try to give his village congregation an overall view of biblical history and literature. Much of this seems rather dull and pedestrian today, but it is nevertheless revealing of his general attitude to Scripture.

The Bible is not one book, but many. It must never be treated as a collection of texts, we must always have regard for the context of a saying or passage. It is the book of man as well as the book of God because fallible and sinful men are its authors, the channels of the divine inspiration. It is a unique book, but it cannot replace other books. We misunderstand it if we go to it for non-religious information. It is from beginning to end a book in which God speaks to us, by his acts as well as by his words (VS pp. 128-54).

Such insights, echoing contemporary controversies of which his congregation were probably quite unaware, reveal Hort's general approach to the Scriptures. We shall investigate this in more detail when we discuss his part in the controversies over *Essays and Reviews* and *Origin of Species* in the next chapter.

Finally, we may mention another series of sermons preached in 1870 on the distinctive nature of the Christian ethic.[7] Hort examines the various relationships in human life, asserting that the clue to Christian behaviour is to be found in Paul's phrase, 'Submitting yourselves one to another in the fear of God' (Ephesians 5.21). The Christian understanding of submission is derived from the example of Jesus in John 13, where the Master washes the disciples' feet. Disciples have obligations to masters, but in the Christian community the reverse is also true. Hort brings out very clearly the reciprocal nature of obligations in the Christian community. Such a principle transforms relationships, presents obedience in a new light, and is the foundation of true freedom; and Hort applies it practically to the relationships between parents and children, husbands and wives, brothers and sisters, masters and servants.

This group of sermons is the only example amongst his surviving sermons of his interest in social matters. Those we have reveal him as a theological rather than a practical preacher.

In May 1870 Hort received an invitation to join the New Testament panel for the revision of the Bible. There was some hesitation before he accepted the invitation, largely because of a feeling that the time was not right with his and Westcott's work on the text unfinished. However, he eventually accepted after seeing the names of others involved and the provisional rules. He wrote to his wife on the day of his accepting the invitation, describing it as 'a memorable day; the beginning of one knows not what changes or events in one's life, to say nothing of public results' (LL II p. 133). His words were prophetic. Over the next ten years the work of revision was to absorb four full days of each month, and a great deal of mental and nervous energy. He was now involved in yet another major project which was to make great demands upon his time and health.

Chapter 4

YEARS OF CONTROVERSY

The second half of the nineteenth century saw the English churches struggling to come to terms with a new approach to the Bible. Two movements of thought in particular made this imperative. One was the emergence of historical criticism, at first in Germany and then in England. This brought to the study of the Bible the same techniques and critical methods that were used in studying other books, and led to the plea that the Bible should be read like any other book. The other was the development of natural science. This raised theological questions about the nature of man and the purpose of life, but above all it brought into question the historicity of parts of Genesis and the traditional belief in the historical reliability of the Old Testament. Together, the two raised acutely the issue of the status, inspiration and authority of Scripture, and put a serious question mark against the traditional view of an inerrant Bible.

During Hort's years in the parish, two famous publications brought these issues into the open, and led to passionate and often stormy debates. The first was *Essays and Reviews*, published in 1859, the second Darwin's *Origin of Species*, published the following year. Both provoked a crisis within the churches.

Hort was closely involved in both controversies, and an examination of the part he played in each will throw a good deal of light on his own attitude to Scripture and the challenge of the new knowledge.

1. *Essays and Reviews*

The *Essays and Reviews* controversy has been well documented, and the contents of the essays frequently analysed. Briefly, we may say that the book consisted of seven independent essays by some of the most radical clergymen in the Church of England, mostly Oxford men and Broad Churchmen, who were wanting to commend to the church the new historical and critical study of the Bible. They were challenging forcefully the traditional view of a verbally inspired book dictated by God verbatim to the writers. They also took the opportunity to air their opinions on other vexed questions of the time—the historicity of Genesis, the substitutionary view of the atonement, and eternal punishment. There is a good deal of evidence of haste and lack of thought in the preparation of the volume, and it is perhaps not surprising that it provoked such an outcry.

> At a stroke the most radical clergymen in the Church of England, save one or two, had apparently made common cause in one book. And all the controverted questions seemed to have been raised together—Genesis, Germanism, Atonement and eternal punishment, the alienation of the masses from the Church, the infallibility of the bible: hardly a vexed topic was left untouched.[1]

It is of some significance that Hort was invited to take part in this project. He received an invitation to be one of the essayists in October 1858. He refused the invitation, and wrote a long letter (LL I pp. 399-401) to Rowland Williams explaining why. But we must not miss the significance of the fact that he was invited to participate. It says a great deal about the esteem in which he was held—he was only thirty, and they were almost all Oxford men, he from Cambridge— and the extent to which he was regarded as radical in theological and biblical matters.

His reasons for declining the invitation were partly theological, partly practical. He shared the essayists' concern to maintain freedom of thought and criticism within the church, their appeal to religious experience as a test of dogma, and their unhappiness with much traditional theology. Thus far he was at one with them. But it was his churchmanship which set him apart from them.

> I have a deeply-rooted agreement with High Churchmen as to the Church, Ministry, Sacraments, and above all, Creeds, though by no means acquiescing in their unhistorical and unphilosophical treatment of theology, or their fears and antipathies generally (LL I p. 400).

The other point of divergence was on the question of authority.

> There are, I fear, still more serious differences between us on the subject of authority, and especially the authority of the Bible; and this alone would make my position among you sufficiently false in

respect to the great questions which you will be chiefly anxious to discuss (*ibid.*).

The other reason for declining the invitation was practical. The project is 'surely likely to bring on a crisis; and that I cannot think desirable on any account. . . I cannot help fearing that a premature crisis would frighten back many into the merest traditionalism' (*ibid.*). Hort expresses his conviction that the quiet unsensational efforts of individuals were having their effect in weaning people away from traditional attitudes to the Bible, and these would bear fruit in time. There was one other reason for his uneasiness with the project. He felt that it might promote the formation of a party within the church—something with which he felt deeply unhappy.

Hort rounded off his letter on an apologetic note.

> I cannot conclude without expressing my very great regret at being obliged to decline so inviting an opportunity for associating with men, several of whom I respect very highly, and with whom I feel that I have in many respects a common cause (LL I p. 401).

We have dwelt at some length on Hort's reasons for not joining in *Essays and Reviews* because they are very revealing of his theological attitudes. We noted earlier the influence of the Oxford Movement on the young Hort. Now we can see how deeply he has been affected by their theology of the church. He could not feel happy to join a group of men who were in reaction against Tractarian ideas. He is not explicit about how his view of Scriptural authority differs from theirs. When we examine his attitudes to the controversy which followed publication, however, we shall see his dissatisfaction with some aspects of their attitude to Scripture.

As for his prediction of a crisis, it must be said that Hort was exactly right. The reaction against the essayists did a good deal of harm to the cause of more progressive attitudes to the Bible. Conservatives used the book as an excuse for pillorying the new theology, and the Broad Church 'party' collapsed. The Church of England, in the short term at least, became not more liberal, but less. Hort seems to have felt that *Essays and Reviews* was appearing at the wrong time, a point made by Ieuan Ellis in his recent very detailed survey of the whole controversy: '"Essays and Reviews" appeared at the worst psychological moment: a feeling of crisis and frustration had built up to explosive point by the late 'fifties'.[2]

How did Hort react when the essays were published? His letters reveal that his reaction was largely favourable. Amongst the welter of criticism and censure levelled at the essayists from theologians and church leaders of all parties, Hort stands out as one of the most sympathetic of all to their cause. In a letter of April 1860 he urges John Ellerton to read the essays, and comments favourably on those of Frederick Temple, Mark Pattison and Rowland Williams. On what is probably the most important of the contributions, Jowett's essay 'On the Interpretation of Scripture', there is qualified praise:

> Jowett is provoking as usual. I suppose he will do good to some in forcing honesty of criticism upon them though there is perhaps not a single thought new to you or me; but his blindness to a providential ordering of the accidents of history is very vexatious (LL I p. 417).

Jowett had made a forceful plea for a new approach to biblical inspiration and interpretation, urging that the traditional belief in an inerrant Bible be abandoned, and that Scripture be interpreted like any other book. We know that Hort was deeply sympathetic with this. It is apparently Jowett's aggressive tone and negativeness with which he is unhappy.[3]

In the public agitation against the essayists that soon ensued, Hort strongly defended them. His reservations about their work were on relatively minor issues. In general, he was behind them in their challenge to the old biblical inerrancy and their call for a new approach to Scripture. In August 1860 Westcott wrote to Hort suggesting he should join in a series of essays in protest against *Essays and Reviews*. Hort's reply reveals his deep sympathy with the seven men who now found themselves at the centre of a public controversy.

> I could not consent to join in any volume of essays which could be plausibly regarded as simply an orthodox protest against the 'Essays and Reviews'. . . I do not know whether you feel as strongly as I do as to the extreme importance of that side of truth which they exhibit. It is familiar enough to us, but there are very many to whom it is new, and to whom it will be valuable. . . The 'E and R' seem to me to *believe* very much more of truth than their (so-called) orthodox opponents, and to be incomparably greater lovers of truth, and a triumph given to the latter seems to me by no means a triumph to what we both hold to be precious truth (LL I p. 428).

Hort is clearly more sympathetic to the seven than Westcott, and firmly rejects the suggestion of essays in protest.

A few months later Westcott made another approach to Hort,

proposing that they and Lightfoot should join in a volume of essays setting forth the 'via media' in the controversy.[4] Hort's reply is very illuminating. He is too aware of the positive contribution of the essayists to feel happy with advocating a middle way. So he writes to Westcott:

> It is perhaps true that I feel the errors of the 'E and R' less keenly than you do. It appears to me tolerably certain that I have a stronger sense of their truths... They happen at this moment to represent the cause of freedom of thought and criticism, and that fact constitutes the greater part of their claim on our sympathy and help (LL I pp. 439-40).

In the same letter there is even a hint that Hort regretted that his excessive caution had prevented him from joining the group.[5]

Eventually, Hort agreed to join in such a project. The book was to be called *Revelation and History*. Lightfoot was to take 'the preparation for the Gospel' in Israel and other nations, Westcott 'the witness of God in His Son' (i.e. the Incarnation and miracles), and Hort the development of doctrine in the New Testament and later (LL I p. 442). Unfortunately, it came to nothing. Lightfoot withdrew, ostensibly because of pressure of work. Hort was keenly disappointed at this, and wondered whether he and Westcott could do something on their own, but eventually they decided to drop the idea.

It does seem that there was a good deal of tension between the three friends in this controversy. We have noted how much less sympathetic Westcott was with the essayists than Hort. At one point Westcott wrote to a friend: 'It would be impossible to find opinions more opposed to my own than those of the Essayists...'[6] We may wonder whether Lightfoot shared Westcott's misgivings and withdrew from the projected essays because he believed the three men were not of a common mind on the issue in question.[7]

We also find Hort trying to rally support for a declaration protesting against illiberal criticism of the essayists. In February 1861 he wrote to Mark Pattison, Rector of Lincoln College, Oxford, and one of the essayists, to see whether there might be joint Oxford-Cambridge action in this respect.[8] He expressed himself deeply worried about the alliance of High Churchmen and Evangelicals which was threatening to destroy the cause of freedom of thought and suggested that a well-timed protest on behalf of toleration might be effective in neutralizing the agitation. This suggestion, however, did not come to anything. At the same time he wrote to Westcott with a very similar suggested declaration, to be signed by clergy of the Church of England, protesting against the 'violent and indiscriminate agitation' directed against *Essays and Reviews* (LL I p. 439). This, too, went no further.

Hort was very unhappy when legal action was taken by the bishops against two of the essayists, Williams and Wilson, for denying the inspiration of Scripture and, in Wilson's case, the doctrine of eternal punishment. When the judgment was announced suspending the two men for a year, Hort expressed the hope that a superior court would overturn the decision: 'I am convinced that now, and for some time to come, mere naked freedom of opinion is the great thing to strive for as the indispensable condition of everything else' (LL I p. 457). His hope was fulfilled when two years later the sentence of the Court of Arches was reversed by the Judicial Committee of the Privy Council.

Hort was, in fact, deeply unhappy with the general negative reaction to the essays amongst both the rank and file and the leaders of the Church of England. Typical was his despairing comment on the debate in Convocation in February 1861: 'What an unreal and absolutely unsatisfactory debate it was in Convocation on "Essays and Reviews"! . . . Surely this wretched paltering with great questions must soon come to an end, or else the Church itself' (LL I p. 443).

We have dwelt at some length upon Hort's part in the *Essays and Reviews* affair because it was a very significant controversy. In spite of the bad timing and the negative elements in the book, it marked a watershed for the English churches. 'A stone had been cast through a window to let in fresh air, and a slow process of adjustment could begin'.[9] More liberal attitudes to biblical criticism and inspiration were now inevitable and the wide acceptance of *Lux Mundi* in 1889 has often been contrasted with the outcry over these Essays thirty years earlier. A process of adjustment and acclimatization to the new knowledge was now under way.

We have seen how Hort was fully in sympathy with the general aims of the essayists, and how strongly he defended them in private correspondence. He was much more sympathetic than Westcott, and perhaps than Lightfoot. He was with the essayists in their plea that the Bible should be read like any other book, and that the old biblical inerrancy should be abandoned. But why did he decline to join the group when invited—apart from the practical reasons we have noted—and why did he remain unhappy with their general negativeness of tone? We sense in all this that Hort felt there was more to be said than they had ventured. But what did he feel was missing?

It is not possible to answer this with confidence. If the mediating essays mentioned above had been written, we should then have his mind on the subject. We have only his mention of a difference with the essayists on the authority of Scripture, but that is not elucidated, simply stated.

A clue to Hort's misgivings about the essays may be found in his comment on Jowett's essay. He remarked that Jowett's 'blindness to a providential ordering of the accidents of history is very vexatious'.[10] This is a revealing comment. It suggests that he missed in Jowett, and to some degree in the other essayists, a sense of the divine element in Scripture, a sense of the supernatural. They had stressed the human element too much.

Behind this lay the issue of biblical inspiration. The traditional view of an inerrant Scripture had no place for the human element in inspiration. It regarded God as by-passing the human powers and abilities of prophets and apostles, so they became mere automata. The divine element obliterated the human. Hort rejected this idea. He saw the Spirit of God as working in and through men, using their strengths as well as their weaknesses. There must be a 'recognition of human agency as the instrumentality by which the Spirit of God works. . .'[11] This meant that there might be errors and inconsistencies within Scripture. There is a most interesting exchange of correspondence between Hort, Westcott and Lightfoot in 1860, after Macmillan the publisher had suggested the three friends should undertake a complete Commentary on the New Testament. Lightfoot and Westcott were not happy with Hort being entrusted with the Synoptic Gospels because he was much more open than they were to the possibility of errors within the New Testament. Hort wrote in his replies:

> If you make a decided conviction of the absolute infallibility of the N.T. practically a 'sine qua non' for co-operation, I fear I could not join you. . . If I am ultimately driven to admit occasional errors, I shall be sorry; but it will not shake my conviction of the providential ordering of human elements in the Bible (LL I pp. 420, 422).

If God used human agency in inspiration, then due regard must be paid to the time and circumstances of the writers. In his sermons and letters particularly Hort was sharply critical of the habit of using the Bible as a collection of isolated oracles. The utterances of prophets and apostles had to be seen against their historical background if they were to be properly understood.[12]

For all his strong emphasis upon the human element in the inspiration of Scripture, however, Hort had an equally strong sense of their divine inspiration. He had a firm conviction that the biblical writers were guided by the Spirit of God. He believed that a 'Special Providence' had been present in the composition of the biblical literature. This is a favourite phrase of his and one used by Coleridge in his influential *Confessions of an Inquiring Spirit*. This conviction comes out especially in the correspondence over the 1860 Commentary scheme mentioned above. Hort, under attack from his friends, professed to having a 'strong sense of the Divine purpose guiding all its (i.e. the New Testament's) parts', and claimed 'I do most fully recognise the special "Providence" which controuled (sic) the formation of the canonical books' (LL I pp. 420, 422). If he were compelled to admit the existence of errors in the New Testament, it would not shake his conviction of the 'providential ordering of human elements in the Bible'.[13] A similar emphasis is apparent elsewhere. The Epistles were the result of the apostles' use of their own 'best endeavours' together with 'the help of the Holy Spirit within them . . . ' (VS p. 250). In the case of the prophets 'the divine inspiration does not supplant the workings of his own mind, but strengthens and vivifies them' (AJ p. x).

We find in Hort, then, a recognition of the two factors in the inspiration of Scripture—the human and the divine. Both must be held together. The Bible was the 'book of man' as well as the 'book of God'.

Traditional views of Scripture tended to obliterate the human element. Those advocating new attitudes to Scripture—the *Essays and Reviews* group, for instance—were in danger of leaving out the divine element. Jowett was blind to a 'providential ordering of the accidents of history'. Was this the dimension which Hort found lacking in the essays in general, and the reason for his declining the initial invitation to join the group? If so, a recent writer would confirm Hort's judgment here: 'Perhaps what the essayists lacked most was a sense of the supernatural'.[14]

2. Origin of Species

No Victorian controversy has been more widely discussed, and it may be said, more misunderstood, than that which followed the publication of Darwin's *Origin of Species* in 1860. What is now clear is that Darwin's book came as the climax and summing up of developments which had been taking place in natural science for over thirty years. His work must not be seen in isolation. He took over principles and theories expounded by Lyell, Chambers, Lamarck and Erasmus Darwin (his grandfather), and with the help of his own wide researches set the theory of evolution for the first time on a firm scientific basis. The higher animals and man had evolved from lower forms of life as a result of the struggle for existence. Natural selection was the cause of the origin of species. Man appeared, therefore, to owe his origin to the operation of impersonal and natural forces or laws. Here was a firmly grounded scientific theory which built upon the work of predecessors but at the same time marked the beginning of a new epoch.

The implications of such a theory for the Christian faith were clearly immense. It seemed to call in question the traditional literal understanding of the book of Genesis, and to dispose of the traditional doctrines of the creation and fall of man. The debate which had been going on since 1830 about the relationship of science and religion became much more animated after 1860.

What was Hort's response to *Origin of Species?* The key factor in understanding this is his scientific training and lifelong interest in the natural sciences. Botany was his first love, and at the age of 18 he began noting botanical observations in his diary; a habit which he kept up for many years. Two years later he became a corresponding member of the London Botanical Society and he was soon reviewing books in the *Annals of Botany.* We have noted earlier that he took a First in the Natural Science Tripos at Cambridge in 1851, and examined for it in 1855, and later in 1871. Some of his contemporaries clearly felt he was destined, at this stage in his life, for a scientific career.[15] Geology seems to have been a later enthusiasm, although it was part of the Cambridge Tripos. It will be recalled that, during the two years he was away from his parish when his health broke down, he spent a great deal of time exploring the geology of the Cotswolds around Cheltenham. Hort's son mentions a paper that Hort read to a men's debating club on the subject of geological uniformity (LL II p. 184) which suggests he was well abreast with developments in this particular science.

It is not surprising, then, that when *Origin of Species* was published, Hort read it immediately. He wrote to Westcott early in 1860: 'In spite of difficulties, I am inclined to think it unanswerable.

In any case it is a treat to read such a book' (LL I p. 414). He was quick to prophesy that its publication would herald a new era: 'Whatever may be thought of it, it is a book that one is proud to be contemporary with. I must work out and examine the arguments more in detail, but at present my feeling is strong that the theory is unanswerable. If so, it opens up a new period in—I know not what' (LL I p. 416). In this positive, even enthusiastic, reception Hort is in strong contrast to many of his contemporaries within the church.

Hort felt so strongly about the significance of Darwin's book that in March 1860 he tentatively proposed to Macmillan the publisher that he write an article on it, setting out the arguments in more popular form, with criticisms and additional illustrations. Typically, he soon had second thoughts about this, pleading too much other work, no natural history books to refer to, and not enough time, for 'one wants months and months to think and read about it . . . ' (LL I p. 415). Two months later he was still debating whether or not to do it. It was on his mind all the summer, but it was not until November that he finally decided not to go ahead with the article. He had decided that the whole issue raised such complex scientific and theological questions that he simply did not have the time to tackle it. Remarkably, he expressed the opinion that the 'scientific question is a very complicated one—far more complicated than Darwin seems to have any idea . . . ' (LL I p. 433). Macmillan obviously did not give up hope that Hort might produce something for he was still pressing him in May 1861. By this time Hort had decided that an article was quite inadequate to deal with such a momentous issue. 'What I should dream of would be a book, half of it pure science, and the other half theological discussion' (LL I p. 445).

Sadly, like so many of Hort's 'dreams', this came to nothing, as did the proposed article. Of all the things that he talked of writing, these are, perhaps, the ones we would most like to have. We are left wondering what effect on the controversy raging at the time an article from Hort would have had. It would surely have brought encouragement to all those people who were unhappy with the hysterical reaction of so many Christians and church leaders, and who longed for more positive pronouncements from somewhere. What is so sad is that few people were more qualified than Hort to pronounce upon the issues Darwin had raised. Because of his scientific background he clearly fully understood the scientific issues, and his knowledge of contemporary theology equipped him to interpret the significance of Darwin's theories for theology. Significantly, it was ten years later, in his Hulsean lectures 'The Way the Truth the Life', that we see the first results of his reflection upon the whole subject. But we cannot help regretting what a later Archbishop of Canterbury was to challenge Hort about—his silence on many of the burning issues of the day.[16] Nowhere is it more exasperating than here.

Two things emerge in our examination of Hort's response to Darwin's book. First, his positive reaction to the theory of evolution, and second, his conviction that what Darwin had proposed had profound significance for theology. If we seek the reason for his positive evaluation of Darwin, it seems to lie in his conviction that science and theology dealt with quite different phenomena. Therefore, there was no question of religion being disproved by a scientific theory. There is a lengthy note in the Appendix to his Hulsean lectures which sets out Hort's clear conviction that the theory of evolution is, from the point of view of religion, quite neutral. The main contentions in the theory 'leave untouched the invisible conditions without which the smallest change "continuous" or "discontinuous", cannot be accounted for, and therefore the invisible Power from which these conditions proceed . . .

> They contribute nothing to the proof or disproof of God . . .
> They contribute nothing to the proof or disproof of immortality'
> (WTL p. 188).

His reaction here is that of a scientist. It has often been forgotten that all the main participants in the advances of the natural sciences in the early nineteenth century were arguing within a theistic framework. None of them was concerned to disprove the existence of a Creator God. The essential presupposition of their work, however, was that theology and science must not be mixed or confused. R.M. Young asserts that Darwin, Chambers and Lyell all argued that 'the interests of both science and of theology required that their foundations be considered separately. Each could take care of itself and could only suffer from intermingling'.[17] This appears to be precisely the view of Hort, who in this respect stands on the same ground as the leading scientists of his day.

As a consequence of this clear distinction, he had no sympathy with people who attempted to confuse the two in the supposed interests of religion. We see this in a remark he made about Henry Drummond's book *Natural Law in the Spiritual World* (1883). Drummond believed that the theory of evolution could be applied to religious experience, and affirmed strongly that science aided our understanding of the spiritual world. The book was widely read in the 1880s because it appeared to reconcile science and religion. Hort was most critical of it. He described it as 'a quite singularly muddle-headed book', which illustrated what had long been clear to him, 'the powerlessness of the mere love of natural science to teach men to think' (LL II p. 340).

Hort's other clear conviction, that the theory of evolution had significance for Christian theology, is nowhere worked out in detail. Only in the Hulsean lectures of 1871 do we have some hints as to why he believed this.

Firstly, there is the belief that God and the world revealed by the new knowledge must not be separated. In a note in the Appendix to the lectures Hort points out that many of his contemporaries have come to see the two in opposition to one another. 'God and the world are believed by their partisans to be enemies, because undoubtedly each can supplant the other up to a certain point' (WTL p. 217). Some have given up belief in God as a result of the new revelations about the natural world; others felt that they could hold on to their faith only by ignoring that world with its newly-revealed complexities. Both are mistaken, claims Hort. The two must be held together for 'neither can really be loved without the other. Self is the one rival of both, which takes advantage of all exclusive devotion to either' (*ibid.*). And he writes of a 'twofold veil' which 'has been withdrawn from before our eyes: the world has been discovered to us and God has been discovered to us. Neither can now be relinquished . . . account has to be taken of them in all things. . . There is no safety but in the full accepting of both in open daylight' (WTL p. 216).

Then, there is the suggestion that the growing knowledge of the natural order is a necessary complement to man's eternal quest for knowledge of God. The danger of the latter was that it tended to be purely speculative. What Hort terms the 'elder' knowledge (in contrast to the 'younger') 'was itself imperfect, and always tending to become the shadow of a once substantial knowledge, so long as the younger was unborn; and it failed at last to maintain that power over life and action without which the conventional honour which it received was vain' (WTL p. 80). The new knowledge of the earth and its history will inevitably help to 'earth' men's theological speculations.

Hort almost seems to believe that the findings of natural science are necessary for a true understanding of the Christian gospel itself.

'It is not too much to say', he asserts, 'that the Gospel itself can never be fully known till nature as well as man is fully known; and that the manifestation of nature as well as man in Christ is part of His manifestation of God' (WTL p. 83). He advocates the revival of the Logos doctrine to express this unity of nature and grace in Christ (WTL pp. 214-15).

Another of his cryptic appended notes to these lectures suggests that the new knowledge may revive the belief, precious to the eastern theological tradition, of a sacramental universe. 'All Christian life is sacramental. Not alone in our highest acts of Communion are we partaking of heavenly powers through earthly signs and vehicles. This neglected faith may be revived through increased sympathy with the earth derived from fuller knowledge, through the fearless love of all things' (WTL p. 213). These are the words of a man whose faith was constantly nourished by his observations of the natural world, botanical expeditions and fossil-collecting outings. In his lecture on Jesus' words 'I am the Truth', he makes clear that the primary foundation of the Christian faith is the life, death and resurrection of Jesus, and what men have done and taught in obedience to him. Then he adds: 'But the earth as well as the heaven is full of God's glory, and His visible glory is but the garment of His truth; so that every addition to truth becomes a fresh opportunity for adoration' (WTL pp. 84-85). Here again is that emphasis on God's revelation in nature as well as grace we noted earlier, a revelation which the new findings had underlined.

The other insight Hort clearly articulates concerns man's nature. If the new discoveries had brought a deeper understanding of God's relationship with the natural world, they had also brought a deeper insight into the nature of man. Evolution had brought home to us our kinship with the whole world of nature. Previously, theology had seen man as standing over and against nature. That could no longer be true. He is now part of nature, no longer 'an independent being, severed by an impassable chasm from all lower things, and therefore able to pursue a separate perfection' (WTL p. 82). Men must now feel 'a true kinship to the earth and to all that lives upon it' (WTL p. 81). He is no longer distinct and separate from the rest of creation. Hort realizes the ambiguity of this new realization, how it brings with it a challenge to the Christian estimate of man. He foresees that there will be a greater temptation for human beings 'to judge of ourselves and all that is above us by measures and procedures taken exclusively from things below us' (WTL p. 82). Here, the Christian must remember the other aspect of God's revelation, that in Christ, which reminds him that he is no mere animal, but has a special dignity which distinguishes him and is bestowed on him by Christ (WTL p. 83).

None of these insights is developed very fully, but they do show us that Hort firmly believed the new science had profound relevance for theology and must have some bearing on the theologian's articulation of his vision.

Hort's overall response, then, to *Origin of Species* was very positive. In this he stands in clear contrast to many of his contemporaries within the church. As with *Essays and Reviews*, he is one of a minority which fully understands the issues involved and sees the need for Christians to adjust to new truth. When Charles Darwin took an honorary degree at Cambridge in 1877, Hort dined in the evening with the Philosophical Society to meet Darwin and a distinguished gathering of scientists. Seventeen years after publication of the celebrated book, he clearly still retained his respect for its author.

Today, the two controversies surrounding the publication of *Essays and Reviews* and *Origin of Species* seem far distant and remote from our time. The truth is otherwise. The past two or three decades have seen a new debate in Catholic and Protestant circles on the authority and inspiration of Scripture, and the emergence of hermeneutics as a central concern in biblical scholarship. There has also in recent years been a re-examination of Darwin's theory of evolution and its relationship to biblical attitudes and doctrines. The strong revival of Protestant fundamentalism has been one factor in the reassertion of traditional attitudes to Scripture, and the re-examination of what were once thought to be assured conclusions.

All this gives quite fresh significance to the attitudes of people like Hort, who faced these issues when they were first raised most acutely, and who worked quietly to wean the church away from traditional attitudes and to face the challenge of new truth. Contemporary debates on the status and authority of the Bible, Darwinism and creationism give a new relevance to his speculations.

3. *The Way the Truth the Life*

Hort's Hulsean lectures of 1871 are his only published contribution in the field of Christian apologetics, which he claimed late in his life was his central concern. They were revised and re-written after delivery but never completed, and they were not in fact published till after his death in 1893.

They are arguably his most important work, for as we have seen in outlining Hort's response to the Darwin controversy, they contain the results of his reflection upon the theological controversies which raged throughout the 1860s. That is why it is appropriate to deal with them here. A brief outline will indicate their scope and relevance to the two controversies which have concerned us in this chapter, and to other contemporary debates.

The lectures consist of a kind of sustained theological meditation on the words of Jesus in John 14.5-6.[18] The biblical exegesis is clear and precise, but the words of Jesus are used as a starting-point to range over a wide field of theological issues. Each lecture shows the significance of the words of Jesus for the disciples and early Christians, and then attempts to relate them to the contemporary situation.

The first lecture deals with the claim of Jesus, 'I am the Way' (WTL pp. 3-40). This is interpreted as a claim to be both the way to God and the way which men must follow. The disciples had inherited a belief that God had provided the 'way' for them in the Old Covenant, but this had lost its former hold over men, and there was a need for a quite new revelation of the way of God. This the disciples found in Christ. In their experience they discovered him to be the way in both senses, and this led them in time to acknowledge him as the universal way of God for all men. This experience is set down in Acts, where the Christian life is actually described as 'the Way', and in the Epistles, which bear witness to the one way of the Incarnate Lord.

Hort relates this claim to the widespread sense in the contemporary church of the passing away of a 'Christian world' (we would say 'Christendom'). This is a crisis like that which faced the disciples when Jesus announced his imminent departure. At such a time the church must have faith that he is leading it on to a deeper faith in his universality and sovereignty. The uncertainty of the future need not be feared, for running through past and future alike is the one way of Him who is 'the same yesterday, today and for ever', and the same Spirit will be present as guide.

Hort frequently speaks in these lectures of the crisis facing the church of his day. This particular one, the awareness of the break-up of Christendom, and the alienation of the churches from the vast majority of people, he would refer to again.[19] Here we note the refusal to regret the passing of the old order and the confidence that the church was being led on through its uncertainty to something new and more fruitful.

The second lecture examines Christ's claim to be 'the Truth' (WTL pp. 41-94). This is the finest of the four, without question. Hort argues that Christianity broke new ground in the central place it gave to truth, showing that the pursuit and knowledge of truth is an essential part of Christian worship and discipleship. This truth was embodied in the person of Christ. Of all the evangelists, it is John who most clearly presents the gospel as a revelation of truth. The emphasis is there also, however, in the church's proclamation in Acts, and in the later letters of St Paul, and those of John. In the later history of the church, it is in the great creative periods of the Alexandrian church and the Middle Ages that the conviction shone most clearly that the gospel is 'a message not merely of salvation but of truth, touching and blessing and vivifying all other truth . . .' (WTL p. 72). Only in the last five centuries, however, has it been realized that theological truth is not the only type of truth, and other types of knowledge have taken their place alongside theology, to the enrichment of the latter.

When he turns to apply this in the contemporary setting, Hort has foremost in his mind the challenge of the growth of science to the Christian concept of truth. We have already noted some of his insights here in our discussion of his reaction to *Origin of Species*. He will not have sharp lines drawn between theological and other truth, for revealed truth is not different in kind from discovered truth. For the Christian, the unity of all truth is to be seen in Him who claimed to be 'the Truth'. Hort welcomes the great strides being made in the study of the natural world, because theological truth is necessarily incomplete without knowledge of the world around us. All truth enriches our knowledge of God and the gospel of Christ, so the Christian need have no fear of new forms of knowledge. The current challenge to the church is to 'carry that light which alone is the light of life into all the outlying worlds of knowledge as of action and of life' (WTL p. 88).

The closing pages of this lecture are some of the most moving and profound ever written by Hort. In them, he speaks of the dangers and difficulties inherent in the current challenges to the church, of how this may involve the surrender of parts of our heritage, and will lead to some losing their faith altogether. Those challenges have nevertheless to be faced fearlessly for 'no faith founded on truth can ever die except that it may rise to a better life' (WTL p. 89). Clearly he has in mind here not only the Darwin controversy, but also that initiated by *Essays and Reviews* centring on the authority and inspiration of Scripture. Hort also makes the profound point that truth is apprehended not just through our intellectual faculties; it has a moral dimension, and the pursuit of truth is a moral and spiritual discipline, not a mere academic exercise. It depends on the quality of life of the seeker.

There are numerous references in this lecture to the place of tradition in the church's life. The scientific method is inherently distrustful of tradition. Hort, however, is at pains to show that the history and tradition of the church have a very important rôle in the church's life, and that we must not accept the current view that truth is only to be found in what we have proved for ourselves.[20] Here again we find that emphasis in Hort we have noted before, what we may term his 'both . . . and . . . ' insistence. Theological and scientific truth must not be opposed to one another, but reconciled. They are part of the one pursuit of truth.

The third lecture reflects on the words 'I am the Life' (WTL pp. 95-149). Lectures 3 and 4 were never completed for publication by Hort, and consequently are less satisfactory than 1 and 2. The discussion on 'I am the Life' concentrates almost entirely on its New Testament context, and little space is given to its relevance in the contemporary situation. Hort traces the concept of life through Judaism and the older religions, and sees Jesus restoring this concept in his teaching, through his insistence on a new quality of life available through him. For him life is 'the ultimate and fundamental form of human good, the highest and the deepest blessing which man can in any wise attain' (WTL p. 110). It is in John's Gospel that this aspect of the good news in most clearly set out, and the word 'life' occurs frequently on Jesus's lips here. Hort relates it to his confidence in the face of his imminent death, and also to his claim to be 'the Way' and 'the Truth'. He then shows how life is a central theme in the experiences of the early Church: in the signs of new life marking the Day of Pentecost, in St Paul's emphasis on faith, hope and love, and in John's First Epistle which is shot through with a theology of life. Finally, he returns to the Prologue to the Gospel where he finds the final development of this theology, namely the assertion that all life is one in the Incarnate Son of God.

The contemporary church, like the disciples, is being called to receive Christ as the Life, only not in isolation from the rest of life. 'Christ Himself before long will assuredly cease to be in any sense our life, if we look for His life only in the form of a private affection or in isolation from the lower life which we share with all living things and the varied relationships by which we are united to our fellow-men' (WTL p. 146). The life which Christ brings 'was ordained to purify and control every lower life; and therefore it must enter freely into them all' (WTL p. 147). The church therefore faces a missionary task in a new situation. There is then a call to the individual to accept Christ's claim in his youth, and to join his own natural vitality to the one master Life. In this fragmentary discussion it is clear that once again uppermost in Hort's mind is the challenge, presented by the growth in the natural sciences, to traditional Christian doctrine.

The fourth and final lecture, 'No man cometh unto the Father but by me' (WTL pp. 150-68), is briefer than the others, but is still full of insights, and often sheds new light on familiar phrases and words. After the cross and resurrection the disciples became apostles, responsible for witnessing to Christ's work and bringing men and women to the Father. They were formerly personally attached to Christ, but their discipleship is only completed if in the end it leads to the Father; for Christ, the way, the truth, and the life, yet pointed beyond himself to God. Hort discusses the exclusiveness of Christ's claim here, seeing it as a testimony to the universality of his kingdom which is made clear in the preceding threefold saying. He affirms 'the unity of all things in Him' and the belief that 'when we yield ourselves to Him all things whatsoever that we touch are bearing us onward to God' (WTL p. 159). There follows a fine discussion on the relationship between the claims of God and those of the world, in which we are aware once again of the science-religion debate. Hort reaffirms that the two must not be seen as mutually exclusive. They are only truly reconciled in Christ, who is both the revelation of God and the redeemer of the world.

Hort returns, finally, to the upper room where Jesus spoke these words. His enormous claims then must have seemed empty in the light of their sequel, the crucifixion. Yet it was precisely that which verified them, and showed from the outset that discipleship meant self-surrender. In the same way, in the present, the fact that Christ seems to be leaving his disciples after a time of familiar presence with them does not mean that he is abdicating his lordship. He is rather breaking up an immature discipleship so that it may be remade on a wider scale. The present challenges to the church, and the changes the future will bring, are calling men to renew and make real the faith professed at baptism. With all our humanness, we must daily renew our discipleship to Christ. 'So with all our own inconsistencies and weaknesses and sins we are kept in the One Way, the One Truth, and the One Life; and each step that we take brings us nearer to the One Father above' (WTL p. 168).

This brief summary of the lectures gives some idea of their nature and content. They are, however, extremely difficult to summarize. We have concentrated on the main argument throughout, but there are many 'asides' and parentheses in which Hort alludes to past or present theological issues, which we have not mentioned.

On first reading, they seem to have a timeless quality, and not to be closely related to any particular set of issues. We have shown that this is in fact far from the truth. *The Way the Truth the Life* can only be understood in the context of the controversies which were posing such a challenge to the mid-Victorian church. They represent Hort's own calm, positive response to these issues after ten years or so of reflection. In particular, they embody his response to the controversy following the publication of *Origin of Species*. We have seen how this particular debate has almost become a preoccupation with him. He cannot seem to get it out of his mind, and all four lectures appear to refer to it.

It is worth remembering that the year these lectures were delivered Hort was also an Examiner for the Natural History Tripos at Cambridge. This was a remarkable, and probably unique, combination. It underlines what was suggested earlier, that few people were more qualified than Hort to relate Darwin to theology. While we may regret that the book on the whole issue which Hort dreamed of writing came to nothing, it must be said that these lectures are in part a fulfilment of that dream and that they represent one of the most significant theological responses to the natural history debate of the later nineteenth century.

Some of the best things in the book are to be found in the fragmentary and unfinished 'Introduction', where Hort argues forcefully for theology to be related to experience, and in the 'Appendix'. The latter contains scattered notes which were prepared for, but never incorporated in, the lectures. They reveal Hort's mind on numerous theological issues, past and present, and we have quoted from it at several points.

It is unfortunate that Hort was never able to prepare these lectures for publication, so that they were not published until 1894, after his death. By then, of course, the controversies to which they were originally addressed seemed far distant. They had lost their immediacy and relevance. Reactions to their publication varied. Some found them obscure and difficult. R.W. Dale, the celebrated Congregationalist minister, wrote to tell a friend that he was reading Hort's book. He added: 'I do not quite understand it yet; but I shall read it a second time with the hope of understanding it'.[21] Others were frightened by its boldness and openness to the new thought. Darwell Stone, a leading High Churchman and later Principal of Pusey House, wrote a quite critical review of it in which he claimed only the most intelligent type of reader should attempt it, and pointed out Hort's dangerous unorthodoxy on issues like the person of Christ, the theology of the sacraments, and the relationship between faith and reason.[22] On the other hand, William Sanday, a great admirer of Hort, ventured with some caution to compare it with Butler's famous *Analogy* as a powerful and comprehensive 'apologia' for Christianity.[23]

In spite of Sanday's enthusiasm, *The Way the Truth the Life* has never become more than a minor theological classic, admired by a small circle of Hort's devotees but, like him, unknown outside that circle. It is nevertheless his only purely theological work, and even in its unfinished state is of great value.

Chapter 5

RETURN TO CAMBRIDGE

The inevitable return to Cambridge and academic life came in 1872, when Hort was elected to a Fellowship and Lectureship in Theology at Emmanuel College. This appointment brought great happiness and satisfaction. The burdens of parish life had become quite overwhelming, as had the conviction that this was not his true sphere of service. During his final years in Hertfordshire he had looked increasingly to Cambridge and the academic world to provide a more suitable outlet for him. The offer from Emmanuel was timely, and brought with it a sense of relief.

Another cause of particular satisfaction was that in moving to Cambridge he would be joining some of his closest friends. Lightfoot and Westcott were Divinity Professors in the University, and when Hort moved into St Peter's Terrace he was only a few doors away from Westcott. For the next seven years the three friends were together in the University. The three were working together on a joint commentary scheme, and Westcott and Hort were still working on their Greek Text of the New Testament, so there was a great advantage in their being geographically close.

Another friend he was delighted at the prospect of joining was F.D. Maurice, who was Knightsbridge Professor of Moral Philosophy at Cambridge. Maurice also lived in St Peter's Terrace, and Hort would have lived just three doors away from him. But this particular hope was not fulfilled. Maurice died on April 1st 1872, a few days after Hort moved to Cambridge. It was a bitter blow to the man who had been his friend and admirer for the past twenty years. Hort wrote to W.F. Moulton, the Methodist scholar: 'This is a heavy day with us. We heard this morning of the death of our very dear friend Mr. Maurice. Almost the brightest hope for our life at Cambridge was the prospect of having him for a near neighbour . . . ' (LL II p. 193).

Hort attended Maurice's funeral in London and on the following Sunday preached a memorial sermon in St Edward's Church at Cambridge, where Maurice had been incumbent. For some time he continued as the Cambridge secretary of the Maurice Memorial fund, a symbol of his indebtedness to Maurice.

There is evidence that during the 1860s Hort had become more aware of Maurice's shortcomings. In a letter to John Ellerton when the *Essays and Reviews* controversy was at its height Hort makes a rare criticism of his friend. 'It is at once Maurice's strength and his weakness', he writes, 'that he can approach nothing except from the purely theological side: all other aspects he tolerates and even approves in words, but they remain outside of him. This is an unlucky defect for just the present state of controversy'.[1] This is a reference to Maurice's lack of interest in biblical criticism. As with developments in science, he was not hostile but simply disinterested. He did not regard either as having any significance for theology. Hort, as we have seen, was convinced that both were of the utmost importance for theology, and in his Hulsean lectures attempted to explore their relationships. So in the debates of the 1860s Hort perhaps came to realize that the man he admired so deeply could not be his guide through these new uncharted waters.

There is no question, however, that the two were very close, both in their general theological outlook and in their approach to specific doctrines. We saw earlier how Hort's understanding of baptism was remarkably similar to that of Maurice. The same was true of their view of the atonement. Like Maurice, Hort was deeply unhappy with contemporary teaching which was dominated by the penal substitutionary theory. This, he believed, drew much too sharp a line between Christ's life and death and separated Christ from God. Like Maurice, his most common interpretation of Christ's atoning work is in terms of sacrifice, a metaphor which was biblical, did full justice to the depth and reality of Christ's suffering, and which linked our life with the pattern of Christ's.[2] Such an understanding of atonement was by no means common at the time, and Maurice's views were regarded with some disquiet by his contemporaries. Once again, Hort was sharing rather unorthodox views.

In their general theological outlook, too, they were very close. In his influential exposition of Maurice's theology, Alec Vidler argued that Maurice was responsible for a theological re-orientation, grounding theology in the nature of God rather than in human sinfulness.[3] Hort's letters and sermons reveal that he himself shared this emphasis. As early as 1848 he mentions with approval Charles Kingsley's criticism of 'the central *lie* of Calvinism, viz. that man's natural state is diabolical...' (LL I p. 64). He regards it as significant that the Bible begins with man made in the image of God, and not man as a sinner. Sin is an intruder. 'Sin is not a proper part of ourselves: it has come into us as the mildew comes into the corn. We are to regard it as something foreign to us which we have to throw off' (VS p. 156). He uses the metaphor of sin as a disease in another sermon: 'The Fall, sin, evil, death are here, but they come neither first nor last; they come in by the way as diseases of a healthy body' (VSO p. 89). Hort, like Maurice, regarded God's forgiveness in Christ as a more fundamental fact than man's sinfulness. He saw this truth embodied in baptism, where we are reminded that 'the evil is a filth that can be washed away, and not a true part of ourselves... Here the evil past is cut away, and a new beginning made... Yet we start from forgiveness: the merciful love of God has gone before all' (VSO p. 86). Here we are very close to Maurice's famous dictum that 'mankind stands not in Adam but in Christ'.[4]

Hort's relationship with Maurice has never been closely examined, which is why we have on a number of occasions elucidated the links between them. We suggested earlier that Hort's feeling of being theologically unorthodox derived partly from his close association with the man who had been expelled from his University chair on theological grounds. We are justified in concluding that while Hort never regarded himself as a 'disciple' of Maurice, we see in him one whose theology was quite distinctively Maurician. In our judgment Hort's closeness to Maurice has been greatly underestimated. He is an important link in the chain which was to lead, in this century, to a rediscovery of the work and influence of Maurice, and of his relevance to modern theology.

The return to Cambridge brought the opportunity for close involvement in the life of the University. Hort soon became a member of numerous University committees.[5] His wide interests meant that he was in great demand for a variety of such bodies, ranging from the Geological Museum Syndicate to the Board of Theological Studies. His conscientiousness in attendance meant that a great deal of his time was absorbed in such work.

In 1878 he became involved in a long series of meetings within his own College for the revision of statutes, and in the same year he was appointed for the first time a member of the Council of the University Senate. This was an honour, but also yet another demand on his time and energy. A fellow-member of the Senate, Henry Jackson, has left a pen-picture of Hort at this rather august body.

> I picture him to myself watching keenly the miscellaneous business which came before us, and from time to time interposing an acute and effective remark. His independence of judgement was conspicuous, and his zeal for science and learning not less so. He had the 'free spirit' which, according to Plato, characterises the true lover of knowledge and it made itself felt in our debates' (LL II p. 175).

Hort also enjoyed the intellectual recreations which the return to Cambridge brought. He kept up his contact with the 'Apostles', and attended their meetings occasionally. He attended more regularly the meetings of a kind of senior 'Apostles' called the 'Eranus' which was formed in 1872. Hort, Lightfoot and Westcott were the nucleus of a group which included scientists and representatives from other academic disciplines. Hort kept up, too, his links with natural science, occasionally attending meetings of the Ray Club.

In 1876 he published his *Two Dissertations*. Apart from the Greek Testament Text and Introduction, this was the only theological work he published during his life. The two were exercises for the degrees of B.D. and D.D., which degrees he took in 1875. The first was a minutely detailed examination of the reading μονογενὴς Θεός in John 1.18, in its scriptural context and in tradition.[6] It was an exercise in the textual method he had been evolving in his work of revision with Westcott, and gave a sort of 'preview' of the great textual work that was to come. The preface to the book contains an interesting rationale of the importance of textual critical work, and a plea for the dispassionate approach which uncovers the true reading whether or not it is palatable to different schools or parties.

> To any Christian of consistent belief it cannot be indifferent what language St. John employed on a fundamental theme; and no one who feels how much larger the exhibition of truth perpetuated in Scripture is than any propositions that have ever been deduced from it can be a party to refusing it the right of speaking words inconvenient, if so it be, to the various traditional schools which claim to be adequate representatives of its teaching' (TD p. ix).

The other dissertation was an examination of the Constantinopolitan and other Eastern Creeds of the fourth century, an essay in the history of Christian doctrine. This revealed another aspect of Hort—his historical grasp and detailed knowledge of early church history and doctrine. His detailed study led him to see the historical relativity of all creeds. He found it 'difficult to imagine how the study of Councils has been found compatible with the theory which requires us to find Conciliar utterances Divine' (TD p. x). Even so, the historical creeds are useful and necessary, and 'to those who employ them rightly they are the safeguards of a large and progressive faith' (*ibid.*).

The book was well received by scholars, but because of its rather specialized subjects did not attract attention beyond a relatively small circle of readers.

The first volume of the *Dictionary of Christian Biography* was published in 1877. Hort had been invited as long ago as 1868 to contribute articles on the Gnostics and the Greek Fathers who opposed them—Irenaeus, Hippolytus and Epiphanius. Hort soon regretted his involvement in this, because of the pressure of other work and because, typically, he gave an immense amount of time to researching for it. Lightfoot and Westcott regarded it as yet another distraction from more important matters! In the event, Hort contributed over seventy articles on various Gnostics whose names began with the letters A and B, the longest of which are on Bardaisan and Basilides. Gordon Rupp has described these articles as 'masterpieces', fine examples of Hort's minute accuracy and care in consulting every available authority.[7]

During his six years as a College Lecturer at Emmanuel, Hort lectured to theological students on Patristic and New Testament subjects. He dealt with Origen, Irenaeus, and Clement of Alexandria in the field of Patristics, and his New Testament lectures covered Ephesians, 1 Corinthians, the letter of James, and Revelation 1–3. His work on James and Revelation was later to be incorporated in his fragmentary commentaries on those books, so this is an opportune time to look at Hort's contribution to New Testament exegesis.

Since 1860 Westcott, Lightfoot and Hort had been engaged on a commentary scheme covering the whole of the New Testament. The aim was to provide a new type of commentary which would embody the new approach to Scripture emerging at this time. Westcott took the Johannine writings and Hebrews, Lightfoot the Pauline letters, and Hort the Synoptic Gospels, the other non-Pauline literature, and Revelation. We saw earlier[8] how Lightfoot and Westcott were unhappy about Hort taking the Synoptic Gospels, a disagreement which we suggested reflected a difference in attitude to Scripture between Hort and his two colleagues. The scheme went ahead, however. When Lightfoot's *Galatians*, the first commentary of the series, appeared in 1865, it was immediately recognized as an 'altogether new type of commentary'.[9] Like the commentaries that were to follow it was based not on the Received Text but on Westcott and Hort's Greek text. It took great pains to relate the book to its original context, and the exegesis was grounded in a careful investigation of the writer's grammar and vocabulary. Further, there was a very real theological and devotional concern in the exegesis.

With this ambitious scheme, the three friends were beginning a new era for biblical exegesis in England. They fully accepted the demands of the new historical criticism, and yet at the same time recognized that the New Testament is made up of documents written 'from faith to faith'. Their contribution at this crucial time was of the utmost significance.

Westcott and Lightfoot fulfilled quite a large part of their allotted task in the 1860 scheme, and several generations of theological students have acknowledged the value of Westcott on John's Gospel and Hebrews, and Lightfoot on the Pauline Epistles. Hort produced only two fragments, both of which were published posthumously. The *First Epistle of St. Peter* I^1-II^{17} was published in 1898, the *Epistle of St. James* I^1-IV^7 in 1909. These represent his sole contribution to the joint undertaking begun in 1860! One other example of his exegesis was published in 1908, the *Apocalypse of St. John I -III*. All three were unfinished, and all had to be edited and, in some cases, supplemented from lecture-notes by Hort's friends and former students.

Hort, then, unlike his colleagues, published no major commentary, only these three incomplete fragments. His reputation as a biblical commentator rests upon these. It is all the more surprising that his reputation has stood so high for so long. Scholars writing commentaries on James, 1 Peter and Revelation have often paid tribute to the depth and penetration of Hort's exegesis. In his commentary on 1 Peter, F.W. Beare described him as 'one of the greatest of exegetes'.[10] My own interest in Hort was first kindled by Dr C.L. Mitton, who had found Hort's fragment on James of immense value in writing his own commentary on that Epistle. We can only regret once again Hort's inability to complete a work for publication, and the fact that he did not even begin his commentaries on the Synoptic Gospels. What we would give to have even a fragment of his on these! But there were reasons, which we shall discuss later, why he did not make progress on these.

The Epistle of St. James was the first of the three he worked on after the details of the 1860 scheme were settled. A comment made in a letter of 1862 to Macmillan the publisher is ominous, and tells us a great deal about Hort's approach to exegesis. 'The work upon St. James', he writes, 'which is now to occupy me chiefly, will necessarily involve minute study of the LXX, of Proverbs, and the kindred books of the O.T., and perhaps still more, Wisdom and Ecclesiasticus' (LL I p. 470). It was not until 1871 that he completed the commentary on ch. 1, and even that was later revised for lectures (EJ p. i). His work on this Epistle was carried on over a number of years, and it features among his lecture subjects during his time at Emmanuel, and later when he became a Professor of Divinity.

Hort accepts the traditional view of the authorship of James, that it was the work of James, the Lord's brother by Joseph's former wife, who was the head of the Jerusalem church but not one of the Twelve. He argues that it was writen about AD 60 to Christian Jews living especially in Antioch and Syria. Its purpose was practical rather than controversial, to correct the lukewarm formality into which the community had fallen, and to revive their faith in the face of persecution. Hort also says, however, that the letter was written to correct a misunderstanding of St Paul's teaching. The great value of the letter Hort sees in its testimony to the variety and breadth of the New Testament witness: 'Its very unlikeness to other books is of the greatest value to us, as showing through Apostolic example the many-sidedness of Christian truth' (EJ p. ix). Recent New Testament scholarship has emphasized very strongly the diversity of the New Testament, and it is interesting to find Hort drawing attention to this a century or so ago.

The commentary proper reveals Hort's strengths and weaknesses as a commentator—his proneness to become absorbed in too much detail, which often mars his exegesis, and yet his immense thoroughness, revealing the depth and subtlety present in the familiar words of James. Contemporary criticism had often claimed that the letter of James was a rather incoherent patchwork of ideas lacking an overall unity. Hort's careful exegesis refuted this charge, and showed the 'subtle harmony' underlying the Epistle.[11]

The Apocalypse of St. John consists of lecture notes prepared for publication by Hort's students after his death. He first lectured on the Apocalypse in 1879 and again in 1889, and seems to have got no further than chapter three. The result is a mere fragment, much of it in a literary shorthand. Its chief value lies in a quite lengthy discussion of the authorship and date of the Apocalypse. Contemporary scholarship favoured the view that the book was the work of John the Apostle in the time of Domitian (AD 81-96), or even later. After a thorough review of the evidence, Hort concluded that it was written by John much earlier, in the reign of Nero. He claimed that the work 'breathes the atmosphere of a time of wild commotion' (AJ p. xxvi) which is congruent with the state of the Empire under Nero. Moreover, an early date is essential if the apostle John was the author, otherwise the difference in language and thought between the Apocalypse and Gospel is inexplicable. In an unpublished letter of 1879—the year he lectured on the book—Hort suggests that the very different atmosphere of the Gospel is due to 'many years of soaking in a cultivated Greek world', although the 'Fourth Gospel is in substance Hebraic' and the 'diversity of thoughts is balanced by curious correspondences. . .'[12]

Hort's arguments for an early dating contributed to a reopening of discussion on the question, and one of his keenest admirers, W. Sanday, later admitted that Hort's evaluation had caused him to modify his views on the question (AJ p. iv). In our own time, J.A.T. Robinson has taken up Hort's case for an early date and argued it quite fully in his *Redating the New Testament*.[13] Generally speaking, however, neither this early dating nor the unity of authorship of the Johannine writings have commanded the general assent of scholars.

Apart from this lengthy introduction, the commentary proper is brief and of limited value. There is little theological comment, the notes being largely critical in nature.

The third of Hort's commentaries is the most valuable, *The First Epistle of St. Peter*. He did not begin work on this until 1882, lecturing on it each year until 1885, then again in 1887, and finally in 1892. The commentary contains the substance of his lectures. The fact that after six years of lectures he had reached only chapter two verse seventeen of the Epistle tells us a great deal about his exegesis!

His exposition is based on the acceptance of the traditional Petrine authorship of the letter and its dating in the reign of Nero. Hort does not discuss the pro's and con's of the authorship, but he devotes time to a consideration of the date. He argues that the letter was written from Rome—again, the traditional view—and that its recipients were primarily Gentile Christians. He notes the close relationship between the letter and Pauline language and ideas, and claims that the dependence is on the side of 1 Peter (EP pp. 1-7). Altogether, the Introduction is rather brief.

The commentary proper is the best example we have of Hort as a biblical interpreter. It reveals his thoroughness in examining every possible alternative before passing judgment, what has been called the 'intensity of his scholarship'.[14] This is a characteristic of his exegesis and explains why he progressed so slowly compared with his colleagues. This fragment also shows clearly his theological penetration and his ability to see many shades of meaning in a single word of Scripture. Gordon Rupp's comment is apt: 'He brought to single words the loving attention which he gave his Alpine flowers . . . for him a Biblical word was something from which you might extract layer under layer of meaning—or like a jewel which might reflect one colour after another when held to the light. . . '[15] One reviewer's comment was that Hort had demonstrated the complexity of what had traditionally been regarded as one of the easier Epistles.[16]

This commentary, even in its unfinished state, is undoubtedly one of Hort's major works. Even though the authenticity of the Epistle has been questioned in recent times, no serious commentator on 1 Peter has been able to ignore Hort's work. F.W. Beare's tribute is particularly moving: 'I have found his work of inestimable value for the portion which it covers, and have felt the lack of any equally sure guide from the point at which his commentary leaves off'.[17]

Hort's three commentaries have the same dominant features as those of Westcott and Lightfoot. There is a deeply historical approach to exegesis, which was one of the demands of the new approach to Scripture. This comes easily to Hort with his profound sense of history. The question 'What did this mean for the first readers?' seems to have come naturally to him. There is an awareness throughout of the close relationship between the Old and New Testaments and the significance of this for the interpretation of the latter. Time after time he points out the Old Testament basis for terms used in the New and this becomes the determining factor in translation or interpretation. One notable example is his comment in *I Peter* on the church as the New Israel: 'St Peter, as doubtless every other apostle, regarded the Christian Church as first and foremost the true Israel of God, the one legitimate heir of the promises made to Israel. . . This is the true key to most of the use of the Old Testament in the New Testament generally, and it has especially to be remembered in this Epistle'.[18] There is a massive biblical and Patristic knowledge. You can be sure, when looking at a word or phrase, that Hort will have cited almost every biblical parallel. A comparison of his *I Peter*, for instance, with more recent commentaries shows that little improvement on his work is possible in this respect. The same is true of his Patristic knowledge. His work is perhaps not quite so richly illustrated with Patristic material as Westcott's but his use of parallels and quotations from the Fathers is often timely and illuminating.[19]

Again, like his colleagues, his work embodies a careful and exact investigation of the writer's language and vocabulary. Every aspect of tense or syntax is noted and given its full force, every word is the object of searching thought. His commentaries, like Westcott's, contain numerous illuminating studies of Greek words, which anticipate Kittel's famous *Wörterbuch*, and its method.[20] We know today that this kind of linguistic analysis is inappropriate, for Hort and his colleagues lived before the papyri finds transformed our conception of the New Testament language. Even so, their work made available a vast amount of material on the significance of words in Classical Greek, even if today it is acknowledged that this does not immediately determine usage of the word in the New Testament.

If we ask what is distinctive about his exegesis, the first answer must be his concentration on detail. This is perhaps the most consistent quality of his commentaries—a thoroughness, an attempt to examine every possible alternative before passing judgment, whether the meaning of a word or phrase, or the construction of a sentence. One of Hort's pupils once remarked on Hort's belief that a topic 'must be approached from every side, before the expression of a judgement on it'.[21] This is certainly a cardinal feature of his exegesis. It is best seen, as we noted earlier, in his *I Peter*, where we may cite his treatment of the phrase in 2.6, ὑμῖν οὖν ἡ τιμὴ τοῖς πιστεύουσιν, as an example. His initial comment is: 'These apparently simple words are very difficult' (EP p. 117). Then follows a lucid and exhaustive treatment of the three possible interpretations of the sentence. In his *Apocalypse* we may cite his discussion in 1.10 of the alternative ways of construing ἐν τῇ κυριακῇ. Of the normally accepted translation (i.e. 'Sunday'), Hort comments: 'the facts are not so clear as they seem' (AJ p. 15). Again, the various possibilities are carefully examined.

Unfortunately, this thoroughness was not wedded to a sense of proportion, so that, paradoxically, Hort's greatest weakness is to be found at this point. The same thoroughness is given to issues which do not merit such close attention. Does, for instance, the issue of the order of the provinces of Asia Minor cited in 1 Peter 1.2 merit a long note of twenty-seven pages? (EP pp. 157-84). The learning is impressive, but the attention given to what is not a supremely important question is surely misplaced. This is, however, typical of his work and examples could be given from all three commentaries.[22] Hort too easily becomes absorbed in unimportant details, so that we cannot see the wood for the trees. This is undoubtedly the reason why he made such little progress in his commentary work.

Some of his pupils were aware of this defect in their teacher. One of them, J.O.F. Murray, wrote in the preface to Hort's *James*: 'At times . . . in Dr. Hort's work as in Dr. Westcott's, the investigations of a particular word or form of thought seems to be carried beyond the limits strictly necessary for the interpretation of the passage immediately under discussion' (EJ p. iv). Today, this strikes us as an understatement. A modern historian of the Victorian Church has put it much more forcefully, arguing that Hort's type of mind was fitted for a textual critic but not for a commentator: 'The dry light of his mind lit up every kind of detail and variant. The gift unfitted him to be a commentator. . . It was said of him that he looked through the microscope, not only when it was necessary, but even when he needed a telescope'.[23] This is perhaps a little harsh, but it nevertheless lays the finger on the principal weakness of Hort's commentaries.

Another distinctive feature of Hort's exegesis is his independent judgment. He frequently sets aside the weight of previous opinion on an issue and propounds a solution which is fresh and striking. We noted how in the introduction to his *Apocalypse* he lays aside the weight of tradition and most contemporary scholarship in dating the work in Nero's reign. There are numerous examples in his commentaries of unusual interpretations and translations.[24] Sometimes this led him astray, and we feel that a particular piece of exegesis is unnatural and over-subtle. The impression is given that an unusual line is taken because it is unusual. This is perhaps what Sanday meant when he suggested that Hort's judgment 'was perhaps biased a little in the opposite direction to that in which most of us have our judgment biased, against the obvious and commonplace'. He added, however: 'Just this last reason made it of special value as corrective and educative' (AJ p. ii).

Finally, we must mention the combination in Hort of historical and theological concern. We have mentioned earlier his deeply historical approach to exegesis. J.O.F. Murray remarked on this in a Memoir for Hort published in 1893:

> As an expositor he had a unique power of taking a phrase to pieces, and tracing the history of each of its significant parts, first singly and then in conjunction. Having thus helped his class to an understanding of the wealth of association that had gathered round each phrase by the time that the author came to use it, he would then replace them in their context; and it was often surprising to notice the richness of meaning which this truly historical method of treatment brought to light in passages which might otherwise have been passed over as commonplace and unimportant.[25]

The commentaries, unfinished as they are, illustrate this ability of Hort to enter into the mind of the first readers.

Unfortunately, they do not show nearly so well the other aspect of his exegesis, his concern to interpret the New Testament writings for his own time. Westcott claimed that this was Hort's main concern in exegesis (EP p. xii). Just occasionally we see signs of it, especially in his *I Peter*, where we may mention his fine discussion of ἐλυτρώθητε in 1.18 (EP pp. 78-80). Another memorable example is his discussion in *James* of the relationship between St Paul and James on faith and works (2.18-26) (EJ pp. 57ff). It is only in the Hulsean lectures, however, that we see Hort's ability to interpret the words of Scripture so that they have relevance to the problems and pre-occupations of his own time.

It must be said that potentially Hort was better equipped than either of his colleagues as a biblical commentator. Lightfoot was primarily a historian rather than a theologian, and his commentaries are strong on history and weak on theology.[26] With Westcott, the reverse is true. Hort alone was capable of combining both. It is sad that this potentially great commentator's work was marred by a deep infirmity. We have from his hand only three fragments, which are yet another testimony to the central tragedy of his life and work.

Chapter 6

RECOGNITION AND ACHIEVEMENT

In 1878 Hort was elected to the Hulsean Professorship of Divinity in the University, a post he held for the next nine years. For just a year, Westcott, Lightfoot and Hort were Divinity Professors together in the University where thirty years earlier they had been under-graduates. Their friendship and collaboration antedated their time together in the Divinity faculty, but it was during these seven years when they were together in Cambridge that their reputation as the 'Cambridge Triumvirate' was firmly laid. Their names were now inextricably linked, and an aura almost of infallibility surrounded them. Their students later looked back on these as halcyon days.

They were not to last, however. In 1879 Lightfoot was offered the see of Durham, and after much agonizing accepted. It was a great blow to Cambridge and to theology, but Hort advised him to accept. He was present at Lightfoot's consecration when Westcott preached the sermon. Eleven years later Hort was to preach at Westcott's consecration to the same office, then the only one of the three left at Cambridge. In the meantime, he and Westcott remained as colleagues in the faculty. This was fortunate since they were now in the final stages of their work on the Greek text of the New Testament.

1879 also saw the death of one of Hort's closest friends, the brilliant scientist Clerk Maxwell, Professor of Atomic Physics at Cambridge, and a fellow-member of the 'Apostles' and of the 'Eranus' Society. Hort contributed a letter to a 'Memoir' for Clerk Maxwell which pays tribute to the latter's approach to truth:

> The testimony of his unshaken faith to Christian truth was, I venture to think, of exceptional value on account of his freedom from the mental dualism often found in distinguished men who are absorbed chiefly in physical inquiries. It would have been alien to his whole nature to seclude any province of his beliefs from the

> exercise of whatever faculties he possessed; and in his eyes every
> subject had its affinities with the rest of the universal truth (LL II
> p. 231).

As Hort's son remarks, the same could be said of Hort himself. The latter was deeply moved by his friend's death. He wrote to his eldest daughter: 'He was one of the greatest men living, and . . . one of the best. . . There is no one who can take his place here' (LL II p. 276). We recall what was said earlier about Hort's friendship with people of varied disciplines.

The same year, 1879, the new Cambridge Divinity school was opened, and Hort, like the other Divinity Professors, was given rooms there.

On New Year's Day, 1882 Hort wrote to his wife from Grasse in southern France: 'So that eventful 1881 is ended. Will 1882 be less eventful?' (LL II p. 286). 1881 was indeed an eventful and momentous year for Hort. It saw the completion of two tasks which had absorbed much of his time over the previous twenty years. The English Revised Version New Testament appeared on May 17th, and the Greek New Testament Text, edited by Westcott and himself, on May 12th. The Introduction and Appendix to the Text followed on September 4th. Both publications provoked public debate and controversy. Because of the major part he had played in both publications, Hort's name was central in both controversies. The appearance of these two major works confirmed his reputation as one of Europe's leading textual and biblical scholars. Once again, however, he was revealed as a radical, in textual as in theological matters.

Here we must pause to evaluate his contribution to these two immensely important projects, the fruit of many years' work.

1. *The New Testament in the Original Greek*

Westcott and Hort's *New Testament in Greek*, on which they had been working together for twenty-eight years, began a new era in textual study. Building on the work of earlier textual scholars, they placed the study of the Greek New Testament for the first time on clear scientific principles. The result was to end the supremacy of the 'Textus Receptus' in textual studies, and to set the pattern for all future textual study of the New Testament.

The classic 'Introduction', 324 pages in length, was in fact written by Hort, although Westcott concurred with everything in it. It is a masterpiece of English prose, concise and lucid. In it Hort sets out the principles on which their text is based. He deals first with the basic methods of textual criticism, and then applies these to the New Testament text and identifies the different types of text present there.

Hort's summary of the basic principles of textual criticism is now regarded as the definitive statement on the subject. It was the first attempt in any language to summarize the theory and science of textual criticism, and its conclusions still stand. Stephen Neill asserts: 'No sane scholar would ever think today of tackling the work of textual criticism on any principles other than these. . .'[1] Indeed, it has been acknowledged that it lays down criteria which are valid for the interpretation of any kind of writing—historical documents, for instance—and not solely for ancient biblical manuscripts.

Hort takes the reader through the various methods of evaluating a reading when several alternatives are possible. There is 'Internal Evidence of Readings', which tries to judge what the author and copyist are likely to have written. This must be supplemented by 'Internal Evidence of Documents', the collection of information as to the comparative value of documents. Here the principle is enunciated that 'Knowledge of documents should precede final judgement upon readings' (WH p. 31). This, too, is inadequate without a study of the relations of descent or affinity which connect the various documents. Out of ten manuscripts, nine may agree against one, but if it is found that the nine have a common original, the numerical preponderance is unimportant. Hence 'Genealogical Evidence' introduces a quite new element into the assessment of witnesses, and another principle is set out: 'All trustworthy restoration of corrupt texts is founded on the study of their history' (WH p. 40). This Hort regards as the most important of all factors in determining the correct reading. The fourth critical resource is 'Internal Evidence of Groups', which involves collecting information about the characteristics of *groups* of manuscripts so they may be compared with other groups. The validity of this method depends on the genealogical principle that 'community of reading implies community of origin' (WH p. 61).

Having established the principles of textual study, Hort then applies them to the text of the New Testament. Here he claims to be able to distinguish four principal types of text. Of these, three are the result of deliberate and conscious revision, the other represents the true apostolic tradition and has on the whole escaped the hand of the reviser. This latter he calls the 'Neutral' text, which he claims originated in Egypt, and is seen most clearly in the two great uncial manuscripts, B (Codex Vaticanus) and ℵ (Codex Sinaiticus), both of the fourth century. If B and ℵ agree on a reading, Hort regards this as very strong evidence for its authenticity. The Neutral text is, for Hort, the purest and most reliable of all.

The other three are all inferior. The least reliable of all is the 'Syrian' text, which is seen in its final form in the 'Textus Receptus'. This represents a deliberate revision of the three earlier texts made at Antioch in the fourth century. It was later taken to Constantinople and circulated throughout the Byzantine empire (it is sometimes called the 'Byzantine' text). Hort has a very low opinion of this textual tradition, and believes that 'all distinctively Syrian readings must be at once rejected' (WH p. 119). Almost equally unreliable is the 'Western' text. This, unlike the Syrian, is of early second century origin but its chief feature is a very free departure from the true tradition. Its editors loved to paraphrase, and to remove differences where two passages were very similar. Hort therefore argues that a reading attested wholly or mainly by Western authorities must be regarded with suspicion. This text had its origin in the Syriac church, but was carried to the West, and is best seen in D (Codex Bezae), the Old Latin Version, and the Latin Fathers (hence, the term 'Western'). Finally, Hort isolates a fourth textual family which he terms 'Alexandrian'. This originated in the second century in the Alexandrian church, and is best preserved in the Egyptian Version and Fathers, and one or two uncials. Its text is similar to that of B and ℵ, but it has been modified in the direction of the 'Textus Receptus', and is therefore less trustworthy than the 'Neutral' text.

All this is the rationale of Westcott and Hort's actual Greek text of the New Testament, which as we have seen was published some three months earlier than the 'Introduction'. It is based on a clear rejection of the 'Textus Receptus' as a late corrupt text, and an acceptance of the so-called 'Neutral' text as the purest and most reliable of all the textual families. With its publication, the scientific study of the New Testament took an immense step forward. Earlier scholars had suspected the existence of textual families and one or two had seriously questioned the reliability of the 'Textus Receptus'. But nobody had attempted this kind of thoroughgoing analysis, nor been bold enough to base the New Testament on a text so different from the traditional one. There is no question that theirs was a radical solution, and contemporaries were not slow to point this out.

How do Westcott and Hort's conclusions stand in the light of the discoveries and advances made over the past century? It is not surprising that developments in this period have led to a substantial modification of the picture which they presented. A large number of new manuscripts have been discovered since 1881. Amongst these have been the Chester Beatty and Bodmer Papyri (p^{45} and p^{66}), which date from the second century, thus giving much earlier evidence of the New Testament text than any manuscript known to Westcott and Hort. Moreover, these papyri cannot be assigned to any of the four families which they designated, suggesting that the textual problem is more complex than it appeared to them. Then, alongside the new discoveries, there has been a continual testing of Westcott and Hort's fundamental theses. In particular, there has been from the outset a questioning of their clear-cut view of the inherent superiority of the Neutral to the Western text. This was voiced first, as early as 1899, by F.C. Burkitt, then by Kirsopp Lake, and taken to its logical conclusion by A.C. Clark, who argued that the Western text was the original primitive text, and that the Neutral was a recension of this, possibly done by Origen or one of his friends.[2] This complete reversal of Westcott and Hort's judgment was endorsed in 1924, with some reservations, by the textual scholar, B.H. Streeter.[3] Westcott and Hort's arguments were not to be so easily set aside, however. Their case for the Neutral text was taken up and argued again by J.H. Ropes, who pointed out that it was inherently improbable that a 'shorter' text should have been produced from a 'longer' one.[4] So by 1930 or so, we have two diametrically opposed views of the relationship between the Neutral and Western texts, and scholars divided into followers of one or the other.

It was this impasse which led eventually to a quite new approach to the textual problem of the New Testament. The conviction slowly grew amongst scholars that to approach the problem with the idea that somewhere we have the original text if only we can isolate it, was to approach it with mistaken presuppositions. The central contention in most recent textual criticism of the New Testament is that no one manuscript or family of manuscripts has preserved the original text. The critic must be open to all traditions and possibilities and not preclude one particular class of readings because of a priori views as to their origin. Thus, there has been a rehabilitation of what Hort described as the 'Syrian' textual tradition in recent years, and it has been argued forcefully[5] that it deserves to be taken seriously in the reconstruction of the original text.

So there has emerged an eclectic approach to textual criticism which is very different from that of Westcott and Hort. It discards their principle that the original text of the New Testament is to be found in one manuscript or textual family, and adopts an open-minded approach which considers readings on their intrinsic merits. As a result, what Hort termed 'internal evidence' has become more important in the evaluation of a reading than he suggested, and less confidence is now placed in his 'genealogical evidence' because it is acknowledged today that there are many gaps in our knowledge of the history of the text.[6]

Many questions remain in the study of the New Testament text. It is not certain that the assured results of today will stand for ever. Even though the past forty years have seen the emergence of a quite different approach from that laid down by Westcott and Hort, we must not underestimate their achievement. There is a tendency on the part of some scholars to do this today. Discoveries of new manuscripts have played an important part in the advances in the science, and quite obviously Westcott and Hort cannot be blamed for being unaware of manuscripts only discovered later. There is little doubt that with the resources and knowledge that were available to them, they produced the best possible text. Further, their work has had a profound and lasting effect on all later textual study. There are still notable scholars who, quite against the general trend in textual criticism, uphold their argument that the Neutral text is closest to the original.[7] Its influence on recent printed editions of the New Testament is widely acknowledged.[8] If practice has lagged behind theory in this respect, it is in part a measure of the influence of Westcott and Hort on later generations of scholars.

Finally, we must note that published and unpublished letters throw some light on the relationship between the two men in the making of this text, which occupied them for twenty-eight years. In the early days, it is clear that Westcott exercised a steadying influence over Hort. It appears that Hort was almost sidetracked from the task they had undertaken when he discovered how inadequate were the materials with which they had to work. He found all existing editions of the Versions and Fathers so unsatisfactory that he felt they must embark on a massive scheme to produce new editions of their own. This is yet another example of Hort's propensity for conceiving vast schemes quite incapable of realisation, for to do this would have been a lifetime's work in itself. Fortunately, Westcott was more realistic and he succeeded in convincing his friend that they must utilize the already existing editions of the Versions and Fathers rather than produce their own. A crucial factor here was the deepening realization of both men, as time went on, that the 'Textus Receptus' was corrupt and inadequate. In spite of his perfectionism, Hort agreed with his friend that it was more important to replace the existing text with something better as soon as possible rather than to wait until the perfect text was available.[9]

Another interesting feature which emerges from correspondence between them is their respective attitudes to criticism and hostility. It is often forgotten that Westcott and Hort were doing something which was deeply distasteful to many people. The forceful attack upon their work, and upon the *Revised Version*, by Dean Burgon and others in the years 1881-83 is a reminder of the reverence accorded to the 'Textus Receptus' by a large number of scholars. Westcott and Hort were aware of critical and prejudiced eyes upon them as they progressed on their project. It is not surprising that they sometimes felt apprehensive about the way the public would receive their results. Westcott wrote to Hort in April 1861: 'I feel sure that our text will be called (like B) an 'abridged' edition of the New Testament. It will be extremely unpopular and there will be no means of convincing opponents who do not understand the force of evidence which lies in scholarship and not in numbering'.[10] Hort, too, was aware of the opposition they faced. In November 1864 there was an exchange of correspondence in which Westcott seems to have suggested that even the minor changes in form they were introducing into their text would be branded by opponents as heresy. Hort expressed alarm at this possibility and Westcott seemed surprised that Hort was worried. Hort's reply is illuminating: 'I do not know that I am greatly alarmed at the charge of heresy about the text personally. Nobody in their senses likes it, I suppose; but I can hardly remember when I have felt myself anything else but a predestined heretic in the eyes of others' (CUL *op. cit.*). As we have noted before, this is a revealing comment about Hort's consciousness of being 'against the stream' not only in critical but also in theological matters. This meant that he was less worried than his more orthodox colleague about the way their text would be received.

An unpublished letter of August 1870, in the Chapter Library at Durham, reveals that Lightfoot, too, was concerned about the nature of their revision. It appears that he had written to Hort while Hort was putting the finishing touches to the 'Introduction' to the Text, expressing his concern about the radical nature of their proposals

and asking for some kind of reassuring paragraph to be included
which would play down the changes they were making in the text.
Hort's reply is again most illuminating:

> My own impression is that it is not possible to write such a
> reassuring paragraph as you propose without danger of mis-
> apprehension. All words that could be used such as "unimportant"
> are relative: and after all might it not be plausibly said that a
> revision which substantially alters or affects such passages as
> Matthew vi 13; Mark xvi 9-20; Luke xi 2-4; ix 54, 55; x 41; xxii 19,
> 20, 43, 44; xxiii 34; xiv 51; John i 18; iii 13; v 3, 4; vii 53—viii 11;
> Acts viii 37; xv 23; I John v 7 . . . is not fairly to be called
> conservative?[11]

Hort is not willing to give a false reassurance. In the work on the text,
as in the controversy over the projected commentary scheme, he is
bolder and less perturbed by criticism than either of his colleagues.

One other interesting fact which letters shed light on concerns the
respective attitudes of Westcott and Hort in the later stages of their
work, as the years dragged on and it was still not completed. In the
Life of his father, Westcott's son quotes a 'Times' review which gives
the impression that it was Westcott who kept up Hort's interest in
these later years: 'To Westcott also must be given the merit of having
by his earnest cheerfulness kept up the courage of his shy and
nervous colleague'.[12] Published and unpublished letters, however,
suggest that if anyone needed encouragement and grew weary of this
immense task, it was Westcott. As early as May 1862 the latter is
expressing real doubts as to the value of their work, and his
impatience at the minutiae of detail it involved. He writes to Hort:
'Generally, indeed, I feel very great repugnance to the whole work of
revision. . . Perhaps I think that the result of labour is wholly
unequal to the cost, and indeed too often worthless. . . I cannot
express to you the positive dislike—I want a stronger term—with
which I look on all details of spelling and breathing and form. How
you will despise me! but I make the frank confession nevertheless. . . '[13] In reply Hort admits that he, too, has 'off' days. 'But I am
quite sure it would be wrong to give way to it. The work has to be
done, and never can be done satisfactorily . . . without vast labour, a
fact of which hardly anybody in Europe except ourselves seems
conscious. . . It would I think, be utterly unpardonable for us to give
up our task. . . ' (LL I p. 455). Apparently, Westcott expressed again
later that summer his doubts about the ultimate usefulness of their

project, for we find Hort once again mildly rebuking his colleague: 'About the text generally, I too have cloudy days, but with all am permanently convinced that the work is thoroughly worth doing. . . '[14]

A similar impression is gained from correspondence between them in 1869 about the 'Introduction' and 'Appendix'. Westcott urges a brief 'Introduction' with a simple explanation of what the two have done. He believes that few will read a full explanation. Hort, on the other hand, thinks explanation is essential and that a brief explanation will mislead. Even if only a small number of people read the 'Introduction', it is important that they should be instructed.[15] Later, Westcott asks Hort to do the 'Appendix' as he feels it should be much briefer than Hort suggests and he is not prepared to work on such a scale himself.[16] Then, in 1879, when Hort suggests one final revision before publication, Westcott demurs and claims that his state of mind will not allow it: 'My state is simply this, that I could not attempt to go into revision in detail. I should never again be able to do the work as well as I did when my mind was full of it'.[17]

All this is very revealing, and gives a rather different impression from that of Westcott's son. Moreover, without Hort's insistence, it is possible that we should never have had the long and classic 'Introduction' with its exposition of the principles of textual criticism and the rationale of the Westcott and Hort text.

There is no doubt that although theirs was a joint work, Hort found textual critical work more congenial than his colleague. We have seen something of Westcott's distaste for the minute orthographic details. He once remarked that stops and accents were a nightmare to him, and expressed his impatience at the care Hort took over such details as punctuation and accents.[18] To Hort such minutiae were less distasteful: 'Their dignity comes from their being essential to complete treatment. And I confess, when once at work upon them, I find a certain tepid interest as in any research depending on evidence and involving laws' (LL I p. 455). Here the scientist speaks, as in another letter he wrote to a friend on the subject of Greek accents, bemoaning the fact that he has never devoted much time to their study: 'I can only wring my hands and imitate that eminent man, whom Jowett so unworthily derides, by lamenting that I have not devoted my life exclusively to the study of paroxytones'.[19] Even allowing for an element of exaggeration, Hort's feelings about textual work are clear.

We have digressed at some length on the relationship between Westcott and Hort in the making of the text because the 'human story' behind this vast project has never really been considered before. Unpublished correspondence does throw light on this, and underlines the fact that although this was a joint work, two very different personalities were involved. It emerges, too, that Hort's influence upon the final shape and form of their published work was crucial.

2. *The Revised Version*

It is well known that the intention of those who, in 1871, proposed a revision of the Bible in Convocation was that it should be a conservative revision. There was to be no alteration of the language of the *Authorised Version* except when competent scholars felt it was necessary, and when such changes were made they were to follow closely the style of the original. No changes were to be made in the underlying Greek text (i.e. the Textus Receptus) unless two-thirds of those present were in favour of such a change. Such was the opposition to a revision, however, that only a conservative translation could have succeeded.[20]

Hort was one of those who were unhappy with the original intentions of the scheme. When it was first proposed in Convocation he regarded it with some suspicion, but when he received the invitation to join the New Testament panel, and saw the names of the others involved and the provisional rules, he felt happier. He accepted the invitation in the belief that there was 'a fair chance of a wise revision' (LL II p. 136). Privately, however, he was unhappy with popular expectations of the scheme. He wrote to Dean Stanley: 'The wish evidently is that the revision should be careful, but above all things rapid and popular; and that with this view every discussion and every correction should be avoided which can possibly touch tender points of doctrine. As a mere matter of policy this is wild folly, to say nothing of higher considerations: but such, I am convinced, is the present policy intended'. Of the attitude of Westcott and Lightfoot he adds: 'They are more charitable as well as more conservative than I am; but I am sure they cannot be satisfied'.[21] Hort clearly wanted a thorough revision. He was prepared, however, to suppress his misgivings and he advised Lightfoot to do the same (LL II p. 134). Westcott, also, was invited to join the panel.

In the early meetings of the New Testament company, Hort seems to have been pleasantly surprised at the progress made. There were some members of the panel who were much more conservative on textual matters than the Cambridge trio, but it appeared that they could all work together in harmony. Hort was amazed at the spirit of co-operation within the group (LL II pp. 136, 139). This was not to last, however, for within a year, opinion in the company became divided between the conservatives, led by Scrivener, and the more radical element, who in textual matters were closer to Westcott and Hort. This was no doubt partly the result of the private circulation within the company of Westcott and Hort's text of the Gospels (1870) and the Epistles (1871), leading inevitably to a certain polarization of opinion. So by July 1871 Hort is writing of 'some stiff battles today in Revision', and of the obligation to be present as frequently as possible (LL II p. 146). Later the same year he writes: 'I dare not be away from Revision after former experience of the necessity for both speaking and voting incessantly' (LL II p. 148). From now on, attendance is not a pleasure but a duty, and a costly one in terms of time and health.

Examination of the Registers of Attendance of the New Testament Revision Company shows that of the 363 meetings held between June 22nd 1870 and November 11th 1880 Hort attended 319.[22] This represents about 87% of the meetings, which is a remarkable record if we remember his many other concerns and projects during this period. Such regular attendance was not simply a result of his conscientiousness. It expressed the obligation he felt to represent the view of the text that he and Westcott had worked out over the previous twenty years.

An unpublished letter reveals that in the later years of the revision more responsibility than ever devolved upon him in the battle with the conservatives, and his health was permanently affected by the strain that this involved. He wrote to William Sanday some years later:

> I do not think I have ever recovered from the long strain of the New Testament Revision, especially in its later years. At that time most of the most competent and open-minded of our number . . . were rarely or never present, partly perhaps from loss of interest in going over old ground, but still more from new and exacting occupations. . . Those later years were in great part one long weary struggle to take as much as possible of what full early majorities had appeared from being lost under the two-thirds rule and under the changed circumstances: and the chief burden of defence (I do not mean textual matters alone, for they made up a very small proportion of the whole) unavoidably fell on me. In those late years

> a kind of semi-stupefaction used to come over me some three or
> four days after the end of each session, and last three or four days
> more.[23]

Here we glimpse what membership of the Revision Company cost
Hort in terms of health and in demands on his time and energy.

It is obvious from this that Hort played a very prominent part in
the making of the *Revised Version New Testament*. A critic later
accused him of talking for three years out of the ten years during
which the revisers sat![24] We should remember, however, that his
influence on the company in textual matters was only modest. In the
end they accepted only sixty-four places where they preferred
Westcott and Hort to other texts.

The aspect of the *Revised Version* which has been most strongly
criticized is the English, which is regarded as too literal and far
inferior to that of the *Authorised Version*. It is not clear how Hort felt
about this. His son suggests that he probably approved of it, and even
hints that Hort took a large share of the credit for the very literal
nature of the translation (LL II p. 237). In an unpublished letter,
however, Hort admits the imperfections of the revisers' work:

> I am afraid we have left some misleading archaisms; but I see no
> reason for discarding such as are at once intelligible to ordinary
> readers, and intelligible in the right sense. Of course in this and in
> other matters the final verdict is practically the result of
> compromises which were unavoidable with so large and varied a
> body, and with the supposed necessities of acceptability.[25]

We recall that Hort was not happy with the original proposal for a
less than thorough revision.

As we saw earlier, Westcott and Hort's Greek text was published a
few days before the *Revised Version*. It was perhaps not surprising
that the two should be identified in the famous attack by Dean
Burgon, the spokesman for the extreme conservatives. He published
three articles in the *Quarterly Review*, attacking in turn the Westcott
and Hort text, the *Revised Version* itself, and the textual theory set
out in Westcott and Hort's 'Introduction'.[26] He regarded the two
Cambridge scholars as the chief authors of all that was wrong in the
Revised Version, and strongly criticized their textual work, in
particular their excessive reliance upon ℵ and B, and their theory of
the late revision of the Received Text. In the light of recent
scholarship his criticisms can no longer be dismissed as reactionary.

Hort was the chief target for his abuse, but he never replied to

Burgon's criticism. We know that he thought seriously of doing so on the question of their text being identified with that of the *Revised Version*, which was one of Burgon's main points. He wrote to Westcott that 'the absurd identification of texts should be repudiated, and perhaps by ourselves if no one else will do it, though it would come better from others. . . '[27] Lightfoot urged him not to answer Burgon,[28] while Moulton thought there should be an answer, but it might be better coming from someone else.[29] In the event, no reply was forthcoming from either Westcott or Lightfoot. Hort apparently felt that replies written by other men would be sufficient to counteract what he called 'Dean Burgon's nonsense'.

In retrospect, we may question whether Hort and his colleagues were wise to ignore these attacks upon them and their work. While Burgon's criticisms of their textual work made little impact at the time, there is evidence that his assault upon the *Revised Version* did a good deal of harm, and had lasting effects.[30] A reply from Westcott and Hort might have carried more weight than the replies of less distinguished people.

When the work on the New Testament was completed, Hort was asked to join a panel producing a Revised Apocrypha, and he joined Westcott and Moulton in translating 2 Maccabees and Wisdom. This took twelve years to complete, in 207 sessions, each averaging just under two and three-quarter hours.[31] Hort chaired the panel for the last two years of its work.

Posterity has not been too kind towards the *Revised Version*. With hindsight, it seems that the time was not really ripe for such an enterprise. It may seem unfortunate that it absorbed so much of Hort's time and energy, and affected his health. He himself, however, never seems to have doubted that the task of translating the Bible into modern English was an important one, worthy of the time and effort involved. As early as 1853 he spoke of the need for a new translation of the New Testament (LL I p. 394). And when the *Revised Version* was published, he hoped that ordinary people would now be able to read their Bibles more intelligently (LL II p. 283). For all its drawbacks, the *Revised Version* was a landmark in the history of the English Bible, and an anticipation of the many modern translations made in our own century.

3. *The Signs of the Times*

In December 1882, Hort wrote to E.W. Benson, the Bishop of Truro,

to congratulate him on his appointment as the new Archbishop of
Canterbury. His letter (LL II p. 290) expresses very clearly his
positive attitude to contemporary problems and his fears that the
Church of England was ill-equipped to face such challenges. He
writes to Benson that this is a time for looking forward and not back,
for 'now it has become difficult to think of anything but the problems
of the present, so absolutely new in the history of the world, craving
all possible illumination from past experience, and yet hopelessly
insoluble except in the spirit of St. Stephen's prophetic welcome of
the revolution which was so soon to bring a new heaven and a new
earth'. He then adds a telling paragraph which reveals his deepest
fears about the church and its relationship with the nation: 'The
convulsions of our English Church itself, grievous as they are, seem
to be as nothing beside the danger of its calm and unobtrusive
alienation in thought and spirit from the great silent multitude of
Englishmen, and again of alienation from fact and love of fact;—
mutual alienations both'.

Benson later described this as 'far the most historical and real
letter I have had' (LL II p. 292). What Hort seems to be saying, in his
cryptic way, is that the Church of England, torn by internal
controversy, is in great danger of becoming an irrelevance in the late
Victorian period. It has become remote from the great majority of the
English people; its attitude to knowledge and truth leaves much to be
desired; and the two are linked. Here he returns to an earlier theme
in his concern for the church's attitude to truth, one that we saw him
wrestling with in the Hulsean lectures. It is the remark about
alienation from the people which is most significant here, however.
Hort lays his finger on something which many of his contemporaries
could not see or did not wish to see—the process of secularization
which was under way by this time. It has often been pointed out that
Hort's letter is prophetic, and an important reading of the times.[32] It
shows us that he was aware of the challenge of the increasing
alienation of the mass of the population from the historic church.

Equally significant, perhaps, is Benson's reply to Hort: 'I do not
believe that the two alienations you speak of are *naturally* progressing
on us. They may surely yet be arrested. But what if those who have
insight only prophesy in closets—when they ought to be speaking
from the house-tops? I wish we could get a volume of Essays or
Discourses out of you. . . ' (LL II p. 291). Hort is rebuked for his
pessimism and his silence. The latter was the more telling point.
Benson is here voicing what a number of contemporaries felt about

Hort. Even one of his greatest admirers, Sanday, was to voice it in an article seven years later. The man who knew so much, and had a deep insight into the nature of the times, remained silent on the great issues of the day. In fact, the need for the renewal of the church was a constant theme in his lectures, letters and sermons, as we shall see in the next chapter. But his insights were denied to the wider public who needed them. Here we come close once again to the central tragedy of Hort's life.

It is significant that when these letters were written, the public controversy was raging over the Westcott and Hort text and the *Revised Version*. Hort was very much a central figure in this, as we have seen. This underlines the point Benson was making—Hort was prominent in debates where chiefly scholars were involved, but silent in those which touched a wider public. His silence was constantly nagging at him. In 1887 he confessed to John Ellerton: 'It is always weighing on my mind that want of leisure and freedom from arrears of work have hitherto kept me from speaking my mind on great matters in print. . .'[33] Time was now running out. Hort had only five years to live. It does seem as if his excuse of too much work hid a constitutional inability to express himself in print on 'great matters'. His sense of responsibility was too great.

One of Hort's most time-consuming activities was answering letters. As his reputation grew at home and abroad, more and more people consulted him on matters of Early Church history or more general theological issues. His *Life and Letters* reveal that he gave an immense amount of time and care to answering these. A reply he wrote in January 1886 to an Oxford student who consulted him about the Thirty-nine Articles ran to thirteen pages!

In 1884 Emmanuel College celebrated its tercentenary, and Hort was involved in the various celebrations. In 1886 he lost another close friend—Henry Bradshaw, the University librarian. This affected him deeply, for the two were very close, as Hort's letters to him reveal. The previous year the two men were members of a University Senate committee which drew up a declaration (LL II pp. 260-65) opposing the disestablishment of the Church of England, which the Liberal party were considering at the time.

During his years as Hulsean Professor, he lectured on Patristic subjects, Romans, Judaistic Christianity, and James, Revelation and 1 Peter. His lectures on Romans during the Easter term 1886 (PRE pp. 3-61) concentrate on the question of the purpose of the letter.

Contemporary opinion regarded it either as polemical or as an abstract theological treatise. Hort attempts to relate it more closely to Paul's own experience and personal situation. He links it with a personal crisis in Paul's life. When he wrote it, he was aware of the dangers that would face him on his visit to Jerusalem to take the 'Collection for the saints'—a symbol of the unity between Jewish and Gentile Christians which he had always sought. The Epistle therefore 'could hardly fail to have something of the character of last words' (PRE p. 44). This explains its length and elaborateness. It is a 'summing up of a long and fierce controversy' in which the old feelings and antagonisms have disappeared. Hort finds it difficult to believe that it was written solely for the Christians at Rome. There is a sense in which it is Paul's 'spiritual autobiography'. There is much to be said for this more personal view of Romans. It is surprising, however, that Hort does not make more of the letter as a strategic tool, preparing the way for Paul's mission to Spain.

In October 1887 Hort was elected to the Lady Margaret Professorship of Divinity, a post he held until his death. He stood for the post with characteristic reticence. A sentence in a letter he wrote to Westcott about his candidature has sometimes been quoted as very revealing of Hort's whole theological outlook: 'My one qualification is that I might hope to keep the Cambridge tradition unbroken, and be at least an obstacle to attempts, or unconscious tendencies, to divide τὰ θεῖα from τὰ ἀνθρωπήια' (LL II p. 364).

Chapter 7

THE CAMBRIDGE PROFESSOR

Hort's reputation as a scholar now stood at its height. Within Cambridge he was accorded an unusual reverence by younger students. 'Of the obscurest book we said "Dr. Hort is sure to have it"; of the most perplexing problem, "Dr. Hort knows the solution if he would only tell"; of any subject, "Dr. Hort will tell you all the literature".'[1] His achievements in textual and translation work were recognized further afield. He received honorary degrees from the Universities of Dublin (1888) and Durham (1890), and only bad health obliged him to decline a similar offer twice, in 1891 and 1892, from the University of Oxford. In 1889, in an article defending English theology over and against German, William Sanday claimed that Hort was the greatest scholar in the two countries.[2]

His reputation was certainly high abroad. American and German scholars recognized his stature. He frequently corresponded with people like Harnack and Zahn, and he himself believed that his work was better known on the continent and in America than at home (LL II p. 369).

In Cambridge he was a familiar figure. One of his students later recalled:

> the quick nervous step, the left arm folded across books and papers, the right swinging vigorously across the body as he hurried down Trumpington Street past Peterhouse and the Pitt Press to St. Mary's, or to some meeting in the Divinity School, or as he rounded at full pace some buttress of books in the University Library...[3]

A contemporary mused:

> Why is there no Rembrandt among us to paint that keen, spare face with the grey hair that looks white beneath the black skull-cap, and

> the scholar's beard, and the knightly nose and forehead, all lit up by
> that wonderful grace that only hard work and a kind of self-
> forgetting asceticism lends? (LL II p. 377).

Other descriptions of him single out the piercing eyes as a dominant
feature of his appearance.

His lectures were not popular with undergraduates.[4] His method
was too austere. He would take almost a term to introduce a subject,
and this hardly served the needs of examinations. It was 'too high art'
for most of them. But he was more popular with graduate students,
amongst whom his influence was widespread.[5] One contemporary
attempted to characterize his approach:

> There is something mysterious about those lectures. I do not think
> there is any one in Cambridge whose lectures are so utterly simple
> as yours are; language, ideas, reasoning, everything is simple in
> them. One does not at the time always feel that there is any
> particular depth in what you are saying, and yet, when the hour is
> over, and the notebook is shut, and we are out in our silly world
> again, we find that at least one point you have been telling us about
> has become a sort of living creature in our minds, has made itself a
> home in us, and will not leave off talking to us (LL II p. 377).

Another pupil recalled another dimension in his teaching:

> The bowed head covered with his hands, as we sat waiting for the
> commencement of his lecture, made us feel that we trod with him
> on sacred ground; and his whole bearing was at all times that of one
> who realised a Higher Presence (LL II p. 379).

He would spare no effort to provide references for students who
consulted him on a topic. He was always careful, however, not to
over-influence his students. One of them recalled that 'he seemed to
regard the formation of opinion as a very sacred thing; he refused to
prejudice by arguing with one who was beginning the study of a
subject'. To one who asked him to recommend books to help him
study the Synoptic problem, his celebrated answer was: 'I should
advise you to take your Greek Testament, and get your own view of
the facts first of all'.[6] There could hardly be a better example of the
'non-directive' method of teaching!

During his years as Lady Margaret Professor, he lectured on
Judaistic Christianity, St James (both continuations of courses begun
earlier), the Christian Ecclesia, the Epistles to the Seven Churches,
the Epistle to the Ephesians, and 1 Timothy. He also lectured on the

Ante-Nicene Fathers to the Cambridge Clergy Training School. We shall look briefly at three of these courses of lectures, to illustrate where his special interests lay during these final years. We shall then note two significant omissions from his lecture courses as a whole.

Judaistic Christianity

Hort's two courses of lectures on this subject were edited and published posthumously in 1894, in a book of the same name. They are important in that they represent Hort's response to the theories of F.C. Baur and the Tübingen school.

Briefly, Baur argued that primitive Christianity consisted of a conflict between Jewish Christianity and Gentile Christianity or Paulinism, which was only resolved in the synthesis of Catholic Christianity in the second century. The New Testament documents reflect this controversy and eventual compromise. The earlier books exhibit the hostility of the parties; anything which shows a conciliatory tendency must be late. By this criterion, only four Pauline letters are authentic—Galatians, Romans, 1 and 2 Corinthians. Most of the other letters are dated well into the second century. Acts was written about 150 AD to cover over the conflicts of the apostolic age.

This theory of Christian origins became known in England during the 1860s. It presented a sharp challenge to English biblical scholarship because it appeared at a time when many were burying their heads over the issue of biblical criticism. It was widely believed that one could accept without difficulty all the New Testament documents as authentic and early. The Tübingen thesis put a question mark against this complacent, pre-critical approach.

It was one of the major achievements of the Cambridge Triumvirate that at this critical point in time they took the Tübingen challenge seriously. By careful scholarship, they showed that other, more conservative answers could be given to the questions Baur had raised. They found a middle way between the German and English extremes. Lightfoot led the attack on Tübingen with his *Supernatural Religion* (1874) and the first edition of the *Apostolic Fathers* (1885), together with two important essays in his Galatians commentary (1865).[7] He played the crucial rôle in the English response to Baur. Westcott also played his part, chiefly in his *History of the Canon of the New Testament* (1855). Hort's contribution is to be found in these lectures which he gave towards the end of his life. Some of the heat had gone out of the debate by then, but Hort believed it was still necessary to deal with the questions Tübingen had raised (JC pp. 7-8).

In his lectures, Hort made a careful survey of the New Testament and the early Fathers for evidence of Baur's conflict between two types of Christianity and its later synthesis. His conclusion was that the evidence would not support the theory. The New Testament documents belonged to the first rather than to the second century.

One of his most important points is that the tensions of the Apostolic age had their origin in the life and teaching of Jesus. He inaugurated a new order, yet regarded it as a fulfilment, not a supersession, of the old. This ambiguity in his attitude was bound to be reflected in the Early Church (JC pp. 36-38). Hort argues that Baur has overlooked the significance of Jesus for the later history and development of the church. The later tensions, of which he made so much, are implicit in the bipolarity of Jesus' life and work. As V.F. Storr put it: 'To understand a process of development you must read it both ways, from the end back to the beginning and forward from the beginning to the end. . . Baur . . . reads the process backwards but he stops at Christ'.[8]

Hort carefully examines the evidence of Acts, especially the Council of Acts 15, and Galatians 2, Peter's conflict with Paul, and concludes that there is no ground here for positing a fundamental cleavage between two distinct types of Christianity. The tensions between Paul and Peter and James were inevitable, given Christ's own attitude to the Jewish Law, and temporary; they would disappear in time. He also examines the various Epistles, where Baur had seen clear evidence of a conflict between two types of Christianity, and at every point rejects his arguments. His comment on 1 Peter is typical. Baur had seen Peter as a representative of the most narrow Judaistic Christianity. Hort can detect nothing of this in his Epistle. On the contrary, Peter treats his mainly Gentile readers as heirs to the ancient prerogatives of Israel.

> Here . . . all that Palestinian Christianity represented is entirely out of sight. There is no trace of transitional conditions, in which the letter of the old Law and Covenant has still a certain legitimacy. The Israel of the future is the only Israel in view (JC pp. 155-56)

The lectures conclude with a brief survey of the second-century church. Here again Hort can find little or no evidence of the Judaizing type of Christianity. In his view, Baur had greatly underestimated the effect of Hellenistic influences on the church—a point that was soon to be developed by Harnack and the Liberal Protestants. 'In a word there was infinitely more Hellenizing than Judaizing' (JC p. 193). The thesis that several New Testament books should be dated well into the second century was based on a misunderstanding of the period.

Later scholarship has confirmed the view of Hort and his colleagues that the bulk of the New Testament literature belongs to the first rather than the second century. His critique of the literary basis of the Tübingen theory is therefore still valid, even if his view of Acts as entirely reliable historically would no longer be acceptable, many scholars today recognizing an apologetic interest in that book. In another sense, however, time has vindicated Baur's thesis. The recent discoveries at Nag Hammadi and Qumram have led to a reassessment of the whole question of Jewish Christianity. They have to a large extent substantiated the theory that there was a Jewish Christian stratum in early Christianity. This is now regarded as a distinct movement in the early church, distinguishable both from Judaism and from Pauline Christianity. It is no longer accepted that Jewish Christianity was insignificant in the Early Church.[9]

In the light of these developments, it must be said that *Judaistic Christianity* is not one of Hort's most durable works. Its conclusions are now somewhat dated. It is still worth reading, however, for the calm, unpolemical way in which it traverses deeply controversial ground. In its way it is a model of dispassionate scholarship.

The Christian Ecclesia

This approach is even more clearly in evidence in these lectures, delivered in 1888 and 1889, and published posthumously in 1897. They too cover controversial ground, the battleground of churchmen from the Reformation onwards. Hort again, however, raises the discussion above the level of controversy. One of his students[10] singled out his capacity for working in 'a dry light' as most characteristic of his scholarship, and none of his published works displays this better than *The Christian Ecclesia*. Even so, some of his conclusions disturbed his contemporaries.

The subject is the history and development of the church in the New Testament.[11] Hort's use of the term 'Ecclesia' is a deliberate attempt to avoid the presuppositions and preconceived notions surrounding the term 'Church'. Beginning with the Gospels, he traces the development of the 'ecclesia' in Acts and the Pauline Epistles, concluding with brief mention of the evidence in the non-Pauline literature. The bulk of the time is devoted to Acts and the Pauline Epistles. Almost all the key issues are examined—apostolic succession, the development of different orders of ministry, episcopacy, church unity and diversity, spiritual gifts in relation to ministry, and ordination.

The argument is so compressed that it is extremely difficult to summarize. Fortunately, Hort himself provides a summary at the end of the main conclusions to be drawn from his survey. These are worth listing since they distil the essence of the lectures.

1. The essence of the Ecclesia in the New Testament is the daily life and witness of its ordinary members rather than the work and administration of its officials. 'The Ecclesia as clothed with those high attributes set forth by St. Paul is realised...in those monotonous homelinesses of daily living rather than in administration or business...' (CE p. 229).

2. The locus of authority in the Ecclesia, therefore, is found not in its officials but in its ordinary membership. Hort sees this as the most important conclusion deriving from his study: 'Nothing perhaps has been more prominent...than the fact that the Ecclesia itself, i.e. apparently the sum of all its male adult members, is the primary body, and, it would seem, even the primary authority' (*ibid.*).

3. The offices which grew up in the Ecclesia (deacons, elders, bishops) were the product of adaptation to circumstances, and not the result of any formal designation by Christ or Paul or the community as a whole. 'There is no trace in the New Testament that any ordinances on this subject were prescribed by the Lord, or that any such ordinances were set up as permanently binding by the Twelve or by St. Paul or by the Ecclesia at large. Their faith in the Holy Spirit and His perpetual guidance was too much of a reality to make that possible' (CE p. 230).

4. The authority of the apostles developed in a natural way and was not the result of any formal command by Christ himself. They were in a unique position because of their witness to Christ and the resurrection; they were not, however, 'in any proper sense officers of the Ecclesia' (CE p. 231).

5. The earliest office was that of Elder. It was adapted from the Jewish practice in the synagogues and became practically universal in the Early Church. Their appointment was followed by that of the Seven at Jerusalem, and later by Deacons.

6. There is no evidence of episcopacy in the later monepiscopal sense in the New Testament, for 'the word ἐπίσκοπος as applied to men, mainly, if not always, is *not* a title, but a description of the Elder's function' (CE p. 232). However, the monarchical principle is recognised in a limited way in the unique position held by St James at Jerusalem, and to a lesser extent in the position entrusted by Paul to Timothy and Titus.

7. Apostolic history should be used, not as 'a set of authoritative precedents, to be rigorously copied without regard to time and place, thus turning the Gospel into a second Levitical Code' (*ibid.*), but as a history to be read and applied flexibly to different times and places. 'The lesson-book of the Ecclesia, and of every Ecclesia, is not a law but a history' (CE p. 233).

There are some surprising conclusions here if we remember that the author was a lifelong High Churchman. We recall the early influence of the Tractarian movement upon him, the fact that agreement with High Churchmen was one of the reasons he gave for refusing to contribute to *Essays and Reviews*, and his introducing a High Church hymnbook into his churches when he became a parish priest. Yet here, close to the end of his life, he is putting some fundamental question marks against cherished High Church beliefs. We may well ask whether, at this stage in his life, Hort was becoming more radical in his churchmanship.

Foremost among his contentions was his questioning of the traditional understanding of apostolic succession. He argues that although the apostles were in a special position as witnesses to Christ, they had received no formal commission from Christ. When the book was published this was seized upon and criticized strongly by Anglo-Catholics. T.B. Strong, later Bishop of Oxford, believed that Hort's survey was lacking in a sense of the Holy Spirit's guiding the young church, and deplored the fact that Hort had given no clear account of the stages by which the apostles progressed from being mere witnesses to actual governors in the church.[12] A sterner and more influential critic was Charles Gore, Principal of Pusey House. He was quite confident of the traditional High Church view that Christ definitely constituted the apostolate as the official ministerial organ of the new Israel. 'For the ministry was acknowledged, instinctively and universally, as the divinely given stewardship of truth and grace, a part of the new creation of God ... as an institution of Christ through the Apostles—divine, permanent and necessary ... '[13] Gore argued that the church appears even before Pentecost as a body already equipped with officers holding pastoral authority by Christ's appointment. He could not accept Hort's argument that the apostles had received no formal commission of authority, only a commission to be witnesses to Christ by preaching and healing. This was 'nothing else than an over-subtle scholar's paradox'.[14] In his later work he took pains to show that there was adequate New Testament evidence for his view of apostolic succession. For him, Hort seemed 'greatly to underrate the evidence that the apostles were understood from the beginning to be the divinely appointed rulers of the Church' (p. 691). Another High Churchman, A.J. Mason, described Hort's contention as one of 'those subtle super-refinements which occasionally detract from the value of his work'.[15]

It was Hort's treatment of the apostles, then, which was singled out for special attack. There is little doubt, however, that there were other conclusions which disturbed High Churchmen: the suggestion that there was no evidence for episcopacy in the New Testament; the insistence that the authority in the Ecclesia resided in ordinary church members rather than in officials; and the statement, to which we have not previously alluded, that the New Testament has little to say about ordination (CE p. 216). Another controversial conclusion was the denial that apostolic history should be rigorously copied by later generations. This was a strong refutation of the Calvinist's view of the relation between Scripture and Church government. Roman Catholics and Anglicans, too, would assert that there are a number of binding precedents in Scripture.

Stephen Mayor[16] has pointed out that Hort's conclusions were similar to those reached by a number of Anglican studies of the ministry in the late nineteenth century, all of which taken together marked a 'considerable retreat from Catholic claims for the ministry ... ' It was a period of reaction against the extravagant claims of the Anglo-Catholics. These studies provoked pained reactions from the latter and surprising acquiescence from Nonconformists. It is significant that Free Churchmen have been more fulsome in their praise of *Christian Ecclesia* than Anglicans. We may recall the remark of the Congregationalist, C.H. Dodd, quoted with approval by the Methodist, R.N. Flew, that it is 'the standard work to which we all go back . . . so sober and objective that there is little of substance in it which is antiquated'.[17]

It is helpful, then, to see Hort's study as part of a questioning process, a re-evaluation of the Tractarian and Anglo-Catholic claims for the ministry and church. As such, it has undoubtedly had a wide influence. Some older scholars would argue that this is Hort's most important work. The fact that it is so unpolemical in tone is undoubtedly an important issue in this judgment. Equally important, however, is the fact that its author had marked High Church sympathies. We repeat the question posed earlier: does it indicate a shift, late in life, in his churchmanship?

We do not know. We may only surmise that when Hort came to survey in depth the New Testament evidence, he himself was surprised by some of his conclusions. For there is undoubtedly a tension between his churchmanship and the conclusions of the *Christian Ecclesia*. To take just one example: his emphasis on the locus of authority in the church resting with its ordinary membership, and not its officials. Yet some years earlier, in 1867, he had described himself as 'a staunch sacerdotalist' (LL II p. 86), expressing his disagreement with Lightfoot who in a celebrated essay had stressed very firmly the universal priesthood of all Christians.[18] And all his life he had a very high view of the place and authority of bishops in the church. He regarded them as the real rulers in the church. At a time when there was much discussion about a revival of Convocation, he was concerned lest it impair or modify their authority. 'The authority of a representative and democratic assembly, derived from the wills of individual members and not from Christ's ordination, is anarchic except so far as it is subordinate to that of the successors of the Apostles' (LL I p. 267). On more than one occasion we find him expressing apprehension about the practical consequences of admitting laity more fully into the counsels of the Church of England.[19] We are justified in noting this tension or inconsistency in Hort. It in no way, however, detracts from the significance of *The Christian Ecclesia*, which must be regarded as one of his most influential works.

The Epistle to the Ephesians

The final example of his lectures as Lady Margaret Professor may be dealt with more briefly. He lectured on Ephesians during the Michaelmas Term of 1891, and the lectures were published in 1895, together with an earlier series on Romans, as *Prolegomena to St. Paul's Epistles to the Romans and the Ephesians.*

They comprise a detailed discussion of the authorship of Ephesians. Most English scholars at this time held firmly to the traditional view of Pauline authorship. This had been seriously questioned in Germany, however, and Hort's discussion clearly has in mind their case that Ephesians was the later work of a disciple of Paul rather than of Paul himself.

Hort examines in turn the various arguments against its authenticity on grounds of different theology, language or style, and concludes with a discussion of the relationship between Colossians and Ephesians. His verdict is that the case has not been proved for rejecting the traditional view of the Epistle as Pauline. In his view all the so-called discrepancies in outlook between Ephesians and the other Pauline letters can be explained in terms of the natural development of Paul's thought, language, and style.

This is a very thorough defence of the Pauline authorship, conducted in Hort's usual calm, restrained way. He is always fair to those with whom he disagrees. In a sense, it is a small model of how critical questions should be dealt with. It has been an influential defence. The reluctance of English scholars, even down to very recent times, to see Ephesians as non-Pauline may well owe something to Hort's discussion.[20]

It is a pity that these lectures deal with an introductory issue rather than with the theology of Ephesians. For we must note here that Hort, like many Anglicans before and since, had a special affection for this Epistle. He preached four sermons on the theology of the church, and all four are based on texts from Ephesians.[21] One of his pupils, Armitage Robinson, wrote an outstanding commentary on it. Above all, Hort saw its relevance to many contemporary problems. This is hinted at in his preamble to these lectures: 'In the present day the Epistle has a peculiar value, because in various ways its teaching stands in close relation to some of the problems which cannot now but exercise our minds both in theology and in the sphere of practical life' (PRE pp. 65-66). He does not pursue this in the lectures, but his sermons show how Ephesians deeply affected

Hort's understanding of the church. Running through them is the belief that the malaise in the contemporary church is due in part to long neglect of the teaching of St Paul on the church as the body of Christ, and the importance of the corporate life of Christians. Renewal of the church depended on a rediscovery of this dimension, which was so clearly evident in this greatest of all his letters.

These three lecture courses show us some of Hort's particular interests in these last years of his life. All three were, within the world of scholarship at least, controversial ground. All three gave him an opportunity to examine in depth issues which had long been a central concern of his, but which he had never found the time or leisure to dwell on. All three give valuable insights into his characteristic approach. All are primarily studies in the New Testament Epistles and Acts. Only one has strong theological overtones.

If we look back over his lecture courses as a whole during his Cambridge years, there are two quite significant omissions. The first is the Old Testament. There is no evidence that Hort ever lectured in this field. He appears to have confined himself entirely to either New Testament or Patristic subjects. This is surprising for someone of Hort's wide interests. For it was during his years in Cambridge that immensely important developments were taking place in the study of the Old Testament. W. Robertson Smith and S.R. Driver were spreading the ideas of Wellhausen and the German school which was transforming attitudes to the Old Testament. The traditional literal understanding was being replaced by something quite different. The Pentateuch was not the work of Moses, but consisted of a number of sources of very different ages; the prophets came before the law, and prophecy was more central than law in pre-Exilic times; the Psalms were not composed by David, and many of the Jewish traditions of authorship were untrustworthy; the historical books often conflicted with one another, and their interpretation depended upon analysing the sources and traditions which lay behind them. These were some of the leading ideas. At first they were treated with suspicion, but between them Robertson Smith and Driver effected a significant change in attitude to the Old Testament amongst educated people. By 1892 a large number of scholars accepted the bulk of these findings.[22]

How well acquainted was Hort with these important developments? There is no doubt that he was sympathetic towards Robertson Smith and Driver, and believed they must be encouraged in their work. When the former was appointed Professor of Arabic at Cambridge in 1883, Hort had 'the strongest feeling that the representatives of "Divinity" in Cambridge should give him a cordial welcome'.[23] There was a similar appreciation of Driver's work at Oxford (LL II p. 417). That he knew very little of their findings, and was out of his depth in this particular field, is clear from a number of significant comments in his letters. One, in 1884, is an extremely tentative judgment about the contribution of J.M. Colenso—an early advocate of the 'higher criticism'—to Old Testament study, which reveals clearly how little he had read of Colenso and of subsequent developments in the field.[24] Another is in a letter he wrote to Westcott in 1890, urging him to make a public statement on the Old Testament question (LL II pp. 416-17). Hort explains that he had been prompted in this request by correspondence with Henry Ryle, a former student of his who had succeeded him as Hulsean Professor, who was concerned that a lead should be taken by church leaders like Westcott and Hort in supporting the work on the Old Testament being done by people like Driver at Oxford and him at Cambridge. Hort believed that something should be done, but that Westcott, not he, is the person to do it. He makes the excuse that as Bishop of Durham Westcott's moral authority is greater than anyone at Cambridge, but this cannot disguise his own inability to respond to the challenge of his former student.

In fact, one of the most forceful criticisms ever made of the Cambridge Triumvirate accuses them of a grave neglect of the problems of the Old Testament. In his inaugural lecture at Cambridge in 1927,[25] J.M. Creed argued that the trio buried their heads in the face of the advances we have noted above. 'Hostility to the critical movement would have been impossible to them. They left it alone.' Consequently, they were unable to give guidance to the younger generation of students who turned to them for help on Old Testament matters. A more far-reaching result was a decline in the theological influence of the Cambridge school in the twentieth century, since the guidance so sorely needed came from Oxford, from Charles Gore and the *Lux Mundi* group.

The career of Henry Ryle confirms the truth of Creed's criticism. When he offered himself as a candidate for the Hulsean Professorship in 1887, he received a letter from a local clergyman:

> You are wanted in Cambridge, and I will tell you why. The

> Theological faculty as represented by the present Professors is very
> strong from the Atticising point of view . . . What Cambridge wants
> is a good Hellenist who is able and willing to devote himself
> entirely to the Old Testament. We are miserably weak here. There
> is more truth in the results of the advanced school than any of our
> scholars dare to face.[26]

When appointed to the Professorship, Ryle quite deliberately
concentrated on Old Testament subjects for the next eleven years,
and met with an enthusiastic response from students.[27]

The absence of the Old Testament in Hort's lecture courses is
therefore of considerable significance. The other noticeable omission
is anything on the Gospels. All of his New Testament courses centre
upon the Epistles and Acts, apart from his work on the Apocalypse.
This, again, is surprising if we remember that the second half of the
nineteenth century saw an intense interest in the person of Christ.
The advances in historical method led many scholars in this country
and on the continent to attempt to write the life of Jesus. Strauss had
led the way in 1833, followed by Renan, Weiss, and, in England,
Seeley with *Ecce Homo*, to name but a few. We know that Hort was
interested in these lives of Christ, and read them as they appeared.[28]
There is no evidence, however, that he ever planned to write a life of
Jesus himself.

Along with this interest in the life of Jesus went an increasing
concentration upon the critical problems of the Gospels, for the two
are obviously closely linked. The two main issues, as study
developed, became the origin and interrelationships of the Synoptic
Gospels, and the authorship and nature of the fourth Gospel. We
have seen earlier that Hort took the Synoptic Gospels in the 1860
Commentary scheme, but that he never even began his work on
these. We do at least have fragments on 1 Peter, James and
Revelation, but nothing at all on the three Gospels. The only
significant words we have from him on the Synoptic problem are a
plan for a preliminary essay introducing his commentary which
shows he was aware of some of the salient issues, and the suggestion
that each evangelist had a second source on which he drew.[29] As for
the fourth Gospel, his view was very similar to that of Westcott, to
whom it was allotted in the 1860 scheme. He upheld its authenticity,
and believed it was the theological Gospel distinct from, but written
with a knowledge of, the other three.[30]

Hort's virtual silence on the Synoptic problem must be noted, and
its significance must not escape us. The indictment would be less

serious had he not been allotted the Synoptics in the joint scheme. But the fact that he was responsible for them at a time when there was a growing interest in them, and that he did not even commence work on this aspect of the project, is very significant.

It can be argued that the circumstances of the time led Hort, along with Westcott and Lightfoot, to devote most of his time to the study of the Epistles. Baur and the Tübingen challenge centred upon the study of St Paul, and this inevitably led to concentration upon the Epistles. It can also be said, in defence of Hort, that his interests were so wide that he could not possibly give his attention to everything. There were bound to be some important gaps, and his silence upon the Gospels was one unfortunate result of his involvement in so many diverse projects. Given the contemporary interest in the content and interrelationships of the Gospels, however, it is strange that he should have remained silent about it.

Posterity has not allowed the mitigating circumstances. It has accused Hort, along with his colleagues, of a serious neglect of a vitally important issue. In a notably sympathetic evaluation of the Triumvirate's contribution to New Testament study, Stephen Neill writes: 'The gravest failure of the Cambridge school seems to me to have been its neglect of the problems of the Synoptic Gospels and of the life of Christ'.[31] It is a verdict which others have shared.[32] In 1898 one of Hort's former students could say of the Synoptic problem: 'In England so far as published work is concerned we are at the very beginning—the foundations of the study have not yet been laid'.[33] Yet work on this had been going on for the previous thirty years at least. The lack of guidance from Cambridge was, like their neglect of the Old Testament issue, to have lasting effects. Leadership in this vital field was to pass to Oxford, where Sanday and his Oxford seminar prepared the ground for Streeter to revolutionize the study of the whole subject.

Chapter 8

THE PARTING OF FRIENDS

Hort's final years brought increased ill-health, and the final break-up of the Triumvirate. There were also painful reminders of the things he had failed to achieve. There were memories, too. In June 1888 he revisited his birthplace, Dublin, for the first time for over fifty years, and in January 1889 Cheltenham, where he had lived as a child.

The break-up of the Triumvirate came with the death of Lightfoot on December 20th 1889. This was a great blow to Hort. He had visited his friend during his final illness in January, when he had seemed better, but it was only a temporary rally. His account of the funeral, with the journey to Auckland and the homage of the Durham people, is deeply moving (LL II pp. 409-10). Perhaps the most poignant moment was when he and Westcott 'stood in the chapel of Auckland Castle, looking together into the open grave of the youngest of "the three", and the first to be removed' (LL II p. 370).

Hort paid tribute to his friend in the article he wrote about him for the *Dictionary of National Biography*, completed just three weeks before his own death in November 1892.[1] It contains warm appreciation of his achievements as a New Testament scholar and commentator, but is also an honest and shrewd revelation of his weaknesses. Of Lightfoot's commentaries he remarks: 'The prevailing characteristic is masculine good sense unaccompanied by either the insight or the delusion of subtlety'. Of his unphilosophical cast of mind he writes: 'By mental habit he shrank from what seemed to him abstract speculation' (pp. 237, 238). In a letter to Westcott written soon after Lightfoot's death, Hort claimed that the latter's love of concrete facts and distaste for generalisation and speculation was typically English, and this explained his immense popularity with the English public. 'But would it not be a pity to seem to suggest that the region which had little attraction for him is, in itself, barren cloudland, as so many people assure us it is'? (LL II p. 411). This confirms what we suggested earlier, that within the Triumvirate Hort was closer to Westcott because of a temperamental similarity of mind.

1889 also brought sadness and pain of a different kind. In July of that year, one of Hort's warmest admirers, W. Sanday, wrote an article in the *Contemporary Review* in which he appealed to Hort to speak out publicly on some of the burning issues of the day. He compared him with Achilles sitting in his tent and refusing to go down into the battle.[2] The criticism touched an exposed nerve. Hort had long been aware of his silence in this respect, and only seven years earlier the Archbishop of Canterbury had made the same challenge to him.[3]

In his reply, Hort makes the confession that he had been forced to spend much of his life on projects which lay outside his principal field of interest.

> It is only by accident, so to speak, that I have had to occupy myself with texts, literary and historical criticism, or even exegesis of Scripture. What from earliest manhood I have most cared for, and what I have at all times most longed to have the faculty and the opportunity to speak about, is what one may call fundamental doctrine, alike on its speculative and on its historical side, and especially the relations of the Gospel to the Jewish and Gentile 'Preparations', and its permanent relations to all human knowledge and action (LL II p. 406).

Hort is really saying, in his defence, that his main concern was with theological rather than with critical questions, and that it was purely by accident, and not by choice, that so much of his time had been given to critical matters. It was this, more than anything else, which had prevented him from speaking out as Sanday and others wanted him to do.

How seriously should we take Hort's defence of himself here? Was he really being honest or was he deceiving himself? There is little doubt that Hort enjoyed, and was temperamentally suited to, the minute textual and exegetical work which exacted so much of his time and energy. We saw in our discussion of the making of the Greek Text of the New Testament how Hort found this much more congenial work than Westcott, and how he had to keep up the latter's interest in the final years. The remark about devoting his life to the study of Greek accents,[4] however seriously or otherwise we take it, surely betrays an intense love of this kind of work. Hort once received a letter from Tregelles, another textual critic, which expressed the feeling many had that he was wasting his time in such an esoteric study. 'On every side I am looked on by those with whom I meet as a kind of dreamer, who have given up my life to a vain pursuit, just as profitless as would be the following of shadows. I am therefore glad to be sometimes in contact with some who at least understand what I intend'.[5] It is significant that he could write to Hort as one who rejected the popular estimation of textual work as a waste of time.

If Hort cared more for critical work than he admits, it is also true that when the opportunities came to write or speak out on theological matters, he rarely ever took them. The debate over *Origin of Species* is a classic example. The article and book, urgently needed and frequently requested by the publisher, never materialized. It was ten years before Hort tackled the issue publicly, in the Hulsean lectures. With other issues, the dream was never fulfilled. His letters reveal that at various points in his life he was hoping to have time at some point in the future to deal with wider theological issues, but at present he is too immersed in various projects to be able to do so. When in the parish, for instance, he hoped that a return to Cambridge would give him the leisure to do this. After a few years in Cambridge, he is once again pleading his work is too heavy. The concentration upon great theological issues appears to have been a kind of dream which Hort lived with all his life, but which was incapable of fulfilment. For many people there is always something 'round the corner' which seems more desirable and more important than the task they are involved in at present. For Hort, this was the time and leisure to pursue and speak out on some of the burning theological issues of his time. In his reply to Sanday, we suggest that he confused the dream with the reality, and that he was not being honest about his true priorities.

There were, of course, other factors affecting the fulfilment of his dream. We have noted more than once his perfectionism, which prevented him from publishing anything that was not most thoroughly researched. There was his crushing sense of responsibility, which grew as his reputation and fame spread, and similarly dissuaded him from publishing anything that was not definitive and final. We must not forget, however, that this reluctance to publish was characteristic of other leading Christian scholars of the time.

They knew that the Bible was the 'cement' of society, and that criticism of it had consequences far beyond the mere academic quest for truth. They therefore kept quiet rather than unsettle faith unnecessarily.[6] Perhaps it is also true to say that there was a sense in which Hort knew too much to publish easily.[7] He was too aware of the complexity of so many issues, of the 'truth on both sides'. He typifies the scholar who has an unrivalled knowledge of a particular field, to whom people are always looking for guidance and pronouncement, but who never publishes more than a few articles or scattered lectures. There have been people like Hort in many fields of knowledge.

In March 1890 came the news that Westcott had been offered the bishopric of Durham. He consulted Hort as to whether he should accept. Hort advised him to do so but with great misgivings, chiefly over what the loss would mean to Cambridge and theology. There was also the personal note: 'What remains of life would have to be lived under conditions of bewildering dislocation and solitude...' (LL II p. 413). Hort would now be the only one of the three left in Cambridge and he clearly felt this deeply. Westcott's appointment was another blow for him, coming so quickly after the death of Lightfoot.

Westcott eventually accepted, and was consecrated as successor to Lightfoot in Westminster Abbey on May 1st 1890. He had asked Hort to preach the Consecration sermon, and after a typical period of agonizing[8] Hort accepted the invitation. The time and effort Hort devoted to this was also typical of him. He was up for several nights preparing, and the strain of this contributed to a breakdown in health which was to render him a semi-invalid for the last two years of his life.

This is an important sermon. It is one of the four Hort preached on texts from Ephesians, and its principal plea is that the contemporary church should rediscover the Pauline teaching in that letter, and apply it to its life and practice. This was true, above all, of St. Paul's strong sense of the corporate nature of the Christian faith. 'The most obvious need of all is the need of a conscious and joyful sense of membership as taught by St. Paul, its dignity and is responsibilities, to be felt by men, women, and children, in every position and of every degree' (CE p. 287). Here Hort is returning to a favourite theme. His letters and sermons frequently bewail the individualistic nature of so much Victorian church life, and urge the need for a rediscovery of the corporate nature of the faith as taught by St Paul.

If only Christians would realize they were united by a common faith in a world-wide society, not only the church's worship but the life of society would be affected for the good. So he pleads here for a new sense of fellowship within the church, a sense of belonging to one another: 'a common life, inspired by a common faith; even the common life and common faith of a community of men whose eyes have been opened to the reality and claims of the fellowship which embraces them' (CE p. 289). The fundamental requirement for renewal was that the church become a 'Church taught by the Apostles' (CE p. 290).

There is also an allusion to the need for constitutional reform within the Church of England. 'Sooner or later none could be blind to the imperfection, the weakness, the barren divorce from sustaining sympathies, which must cling to an organisation in which the greater part of the members of the community have no personal share' (CE p. 291). For the past three decades Anglicans had talked of reform within the organization of the church, so that lay people could be given more responsibility. Convocation was a purely clerical body, and many were calling for its reformation so that it might include laity as well as clergy. In the *Christian Ecclesia* Hort had underlined the fact that in the New Testament the church was the whole people of God, and not chiefly officials or officers. This was clearly most relevant to the ongoing debate in question, and Hort was in sympathy with those who urged that Convocation must be modified, and he also supported calls for reform at parish and diocesan level.[9] In this reference at Westcott's Consecration we may detect some impatience on his part that the talked-of changes had still not come about.

The sermon concluded with a warm tribute to the one with whom he had shared 'a sacred friendship of forty years', and a quotation from Westcott's own sermon preached at Lightfoot's Consecration to the same office eleven years before.

Hort was unable to lecture now for over a year. There is much that is illuminating, however, in the letters he wrote during these last two years of his life. A wry comment in a letter to Westcott noted that he (Hort) had sat between Jowett and Liddon at breakfast in Trinity College—this he described as 'a curious experience' (LL II p. 418). Perhaps he saw the symbolism as well as the humour in being sandwiched between the arch-liberal and the ultra-conservative. There is a deeply perceptive letter about John Henry Newman, which reveals Hort's admiration and reverence for him as well as his misgivings about his theology and his essentially combative nature (LL II pp. 423-25). There is a letter about Ammonite fossils to his daughter, and a touching note to his eldest son in which he admits that one of the greatest regrets of his life has been his 'miserable shyness' which has disabled him in his family as well as in his work (LL II pp. 425-26, 451).

He gave his last lecture in April 1892, then suffered such an alarming decline in health that he was advised to go to the Swiss Alps for the summer. For a time there was an improvement, but a further deterioration forced him to return home in September. His condition slowly weakened now. His last piece of work was the article on Lightfoot for the *Dictionary of National Biography*. This exhausted him as Westcott's Consecration sermon had two years earlier. He died in the early hours of the morning on November 30th, aged 64. The funeral took place on December 6th in the chapel of Emmanuel College.

EPILOGUE

Was he 'the greatest of all our names', as Sanday claimed?

Ninety years or so after his death, that seems an exaggerated judgment. His weaknesses are more apparent to us than they were to his contemporaries, and we have not glossed over them. Some he shared with his colleagues in the Triumvirate—the neglect of the Old Testament and the Gospels, for instance. Others were peculiar to him. Above all, there was the deep infirmity which showed itself in a failure to concentrate interests and an inability to publish or speak out on important issues. Posterity must judge a scholar largely by his published output, and Hort published so little. As far as theology is concerned, we do not have the evidence to compare him with Coleridge, Maurice or Newman.

It is nevertheless true that he has been unjustly neglected in the growing literature on the Victorian church. It is quite misleading to regard him as primarily a textual critic, and to evaluate him simply as one of the Triumvirate who achieved certain goals in their common endeavour. Textual criticism was only one of his many interests, and although he shared a common outlook and approach with Westcott and Lightfoot, he differed from them on several key issues. He was less conservative, bolder, much less of an establishment figure than either of them. His theology and his exegesis have a quite different 'flavour' from theirs.

His personal contribution to some of the central biblical and theological issues of the nineteenth century deserves to be taken much more seriously. Quite apart from his crucial work on the text and his contribution to the new exegesis, he was deeply involved in the question of eternal punishment, in working out a theological response to Darwin, and in evolving a more satisfactory theology of the church. The whole question of the church's response to biblical and historical criticism, also, was a lifelong preoccupation.

He is not easy to place in the spectrum of the Victorian theological scene. He is often placed in the Broad Church party, but for all his sympathies with the outlook of men like Jowett and Arnold, he never regarded himself as a member of that party. His High Churchmanship, and his distaste for ecclesiastical and theological parties, set him apart from them. Perhaps he stands closer to F.D. Maurice than to anyone else, even though he never regarded himself as a 'disciple'. There is certainly a greater affinity between them than has hitherto been acknowledged.

One of the surprising things to emerge from our study is Hort's awareness of being unorthodox in theological matters. His closeness to Maurice is one of the factors in this. Even his textual work is radical in its conclusions, and encounters formidable criticism from conservatives. The fact that Evangelicals and Tractarians regarded him with suspicion may explain why, unlike Westcott and Lightfoot, he never attained high ecclesiastical office.

His influence is difficult to assess. He has been termed the 'Father of English Modernism', but that claim cannot be sustained.[1] His influence is more to be seen in the tradition of careful, thorough exegesis and criticism associated with the Cambridge school,[2] and in men like Charles Raven—a great admirer of Hort—who have maintained a positive attitude to the advances in science and modern knowledge.

Hort touched life on many sides, and maintained throughout his life an unusual breadth of interests. He was not only a textual critic but a New Testament scholar, a Church historian, a natural scientist, and a philosopher. He was one of the last of the 'Renaissance men', before knowledge became fragmented and broke up into specialisms. If this was a point of weakness for him, it was also one of his strengths. It is one reason why he was regarded with such reverence in the last two decades of his life.

He is a significant figure in the Victorian church. If not the greatest of our names, he is surely amongst the giants. He deserves to be more widely known and appreciated.

NOTES

Notes to Introduction

1. 'The Life and Letters of F.J.A. Hort', *American Journal of Theology* 1 (1897), pp. 97-98.
2. A notable exception is Andrew Louth, who in his essay on the nature of theology, *Discerning the Mystery* (Clarendon, 1983), sees Hort as an important theologian, standing with the leaders of the Oxford Movement against the general stream of theology since the Enlightenment. See also Gordon Rupp's *Hort and the Cambridge Tradition* (CUP, 1968) for an evaluation of him as a historian.
3. See my article 'F.J.A. Hort, 1828-1892 : A Neglected Theologian', *Expository Times* 90 (1978), pp. 77-81, for a brief outline of some of these issues.
4. A. Hort, *Life and Letters of Fenton John Anthony Hort*, 2 vols. (Macmillan, 1896); *Joseph Barber Lightfoot*, the Durham Cathedral Lecture for 1981 (Dean and Chapter of Durham), p. 5.

Notes to Chapter 1

1. 'Arnold made me really see the dignity and glory of politics. . .' (LL I p. 132).
2. The form between the Upper Fifth and Sixth, where boys remained until they were old enough to be promoted to the Sixth.
3. 'Inscribed to Bonamy Price. . . in gratitude for teachings of exactness and of reality in language in history and through and above both in theology' (EP, Dedication page).
4. In *Cambridge Essays* (CUP, 1856), pp. 292-351. See below, pp. 27f.
5. *Movements of Religious Thought in Britain during the Nineteenth Century* (Longmans Green, 1885), p. 7.
6. *Principles and Precepts*, H.D.A. Major and F.L. Cross (Blackwell, 1927), p. 170. See also A. Vidler's essay 'Westcott's Christian Socialism' in *F.D. Maurice and Company* (SCM, 1966), pp. 259-78.
7. The writings of Maurice 'have led me to doubt whether the Christian faith is adequately or purely represented in all respects in the accepted doctrines of any living school' (LL II p. 155).

Notes to Chapter 2

1. See Gordon Rupp, *Hort and the Cambridge Tradition* (CUP, 1968).
2. 'Of all the articles of accepted Christian orthodoxy that troubled the consciences of Victorian churchmen, none caused more anxiety than the everlasting punishment of the wicked', Geoffrey Rowell, *Hell and the Victorians* (Clarendon, 1974), p. 1.
3. *The Life of F.D. Maurice*, II (Macmillan, 1884), pp. 15-23.
4. See LL I p. 262: 'his whole defence seems to have been an expansion of that letter'.
5. *The Life of F.D. Maurice*, II, p. 17.
6. *The Life of F.D. Maurice*, II, p. 19.
7. *Ibid.*
8. Eg. A.M. Ramsey, *F.D. Maurice and the Conflicts of Modern Theology* (CUP, 1951), p. 54.
9. E. Abbott and L. Campbell, *The Life and Letters of Benjamin Jowett* (John Murray, 1897), II, p. 305.

Notes to Chapter 3

1. Luke 4.18-19: 'The Spirit of the Lord is upon me, because he hath anointed me to preach the gospel to the poor; he hath sent me to heal the broken-hearted, to preach deliverance to the captives, and recovering of sight to the blind, to set at liberty them that are bruised, to preach the acceptable year of the Lord'.
2. E.g. David L. Edwards, *Leaders of the Church of England 1828-1944* (OUP, 1971), p. 188, describes Hort's move to St Ippolyts as 'an incredible appointment'.
3. CUL Add. MS 6597 (October 16th 1864).
4. The Bishop of Exeter refused to institute the Rev. C.G. Gorham to a Devon parish because he believed Gorham, an Evangelical, denied the doctrine of baptismal regeneration. Gorham appealed to the Judicial Committee of the Privy Council, who upheld his appeal, declaring that his opinions were not contrary to Church of England doctrine.
5. Tracts 67-70: *Scriptural Views of Holy Baptism*, p. 42.
6. *F.D. Maurice and Company* (SCM, 1966), p. 108. The sermon referred to is 'Baptism and Confirmation' (CS pp. 83-97).
7. VSO pp. 107-49. Most of the exposition is based on the 'Household Code' in Ephesians chs. 5 and 6.

Notes to Chapter 4

1. Ieuan Ellis, *Seven Against Christ* (Brill, 1980), p. 53.

2. Ellis, *op. cit.*, p. 257.

3. A year later Hort confessed to an 'increasing love' for Jowett, and said, 'There are things in his essays (not in "E. and R.") which meet the real *ultimate* difficulties better than anything I know' (LL I p. 448).

4. *Life and Letters of Brooke Foss Westcott*, A.F. Westcott, I (Macmillan, 1903), pp. 214-15.

5. 'I still feel they have very strong grounds for their conduct, and I do not altogether trust my own caution' (LL I p. 440).

6. A.F. Westcott, *op. cit.*, p. 215

7. Ieuan Ellis claims Lightfoot dropped out because he 'evidently found Hort's opinions too advanced for his comfort' (*op. cit.*, p. 124). It is not clear, however, what evidence there is for this assertion.

8. Bodleian MS Pattison 54 (Correspondence of Mark Pattison).

9. Ieuan Ellis, *op. cit.*, p. 260.

10. See above, p. 46.

11. AJ p. x (the reference is to prophecy).

12. See, for example, EP p. 57 and PRE p. 124.

13. Quoted above, p. 49.

14. Ieuan Ellis, *op. cit.*, p. 99.

15. Hort's son quotes an obituary notice in the *Journal of Botany* of 1893 which claimed that 'forty years ago Hort might have been styled one of the rising hopes of the Cambridge school of botanists' (LL I p. 178).

16. E.W. Benson, in a letter to Hort in 1882 (LL II p. 291).

17. 'The Impact of Darwin on Conventional Thought', *The Victorian Crisis of Faith*, ed. A. Symondson (SPCK, 1970), p. 26.

18. 'Thomas saith unto him, Lord, we know not whither thou goest; and how can we know the way? Jesus saith unto him, I am the way, the truth, and the life: no man cometh unto the Father, but by me' (AV).

19. In a letter to E.W. Benson on his appointment as Archbishop of Canterbury in 1882. See below, pp. 87f.

20. WTL pp. 78, 87, 91-92. This point is elaborated by Andrew Louth in his *Discerning the Mystery*, which regards Hort's discussion here as an important contribution to an understanding of the nature of theology.

21. *The Life of R.W.W. Dale*, A.W.W. Dale (Hodder and Stoughton, 1898), p. 673.

22. *Church Quarterly Review* 38 (1894), pp. 380-92.

23. In *The American Journal of Theology* 1 (1897), p. 114.

Notes to Chapter 5

1. LL I p. 448. Torben Christensen suggested that this was one reason why there was little interest in Maurice in the last decade of his life ('F.D. Maurice and the Contemporary Religious World', in *Studies in Church History* III, ed. G.J Cuming [Brill, 1966], p. 83).

2. See, for example, WTL p. 135, EP p. 24, VSO p. 228, LL II p. 158.

3. *F.D. Maurice and Company*, pp. 39ff.

4. *The Life of F.D. Maurice*, II, p. 358.

5. They are listed by his son in LL II p. 173.

6. Hort argued that this was the true reading, rather than ὁ μονογενὴς υἱός which had always been the accepted reading.

7. *Hort and the Cambridge Tradition*, p. 13.

8. See above, p. 49.

9. W.F. Howard, *The Romance of New Testament Scholarship* (Epworth, 1949), p. 57.

10. *The First Epistle of Peter* (Blackwell, 1958), p. ix.

11. The view of J.O.F. Murray in EJ p. iii.

12. CUL Add. MS 6597, letter 225 ('The Theological Correspondence of F.J.A. Hort').

13. See pp. 224ff.

14. A phrase used by one of Hort's pupils, Armitage Robinson.

15. *Hort and the Cambridge Tradition*, pp. 11-12.

16. Archibald Robertson, later Bishop of Exeter, in 'Hort on I Peter', *Journal of Theological Studies* I (1900), p. 301.

17. *The First Epistle of Peter*, p. ix.

18. EP p. 7. Cf. A.M. Ramsey's remark that it was not common in the nineteenth century to understand the church as the New Israel (*F.D. Maurice and the Conflicts of Modern Theology* [CUP, 1951], pp. 29-30).

19. A good example of this is his reference to Justin's use of διασπορά in his discussion of 1 Peter 1.1.

20. Among the most valuable word studies are: κληρονομία, ἐλυτρώθητε, περιέχει in *I Peter*; πειρασμός, σοφία, κόσμος in *James*; and ἄγγελος in *Revelation*.

21. Armitage Robinson in *The Expositor* III, 4th series (1893), p. 63.

22. E.g. the discussion of θεοῦ πατρός in 1 Peter 1.2 and ἁπλῶς in James 1.5.

23. Owen Chadwick, *The Victorian Church*, II (Black, 1970), p. 49.

24. E.g. τὰ εἰς Χριστὸν παθήματα in 1 Peter 1.11 he translates as the 'sufferings destined for the Messiah'.

25. *Classical Review* 7 (1893), p. 89.

26. Cf. Hort's comment on his *Galatians*: 'One misses the real attempt to fathom St. Paul's own mind, and to compare it with the facts of life which one finds in Jowett' (LL II p. 79).

Notes to Chapter 6

1. *The Interpretation of the New Testament 1861-1961* (OUP, 1966), p. 72.

2. *The Primitive Text of the Gospels and Acts* (OUP, 1914), pp. v-vi, 106.

3. *The Four Gospels* (Macmillan, 1924), p. 146.

4. *The Beginnings of Christianity*, III, 'The Text of Acts' (Macmillan, 1926), ed. F.J. Foakes Jackson and K. Lake, p. ccxxvi.

5. By, for example, G.D. Kilpatrick in 'The Greek New Testament of Today and the "Textus Receptus"' in *The New Testament in Historical and Contemporary Perspective* (OUP, 1965), ed. H. Anderson & W. Barclay.

6. There is also less confidence in assigning texts to geographical areas as Westcott and Hort did.

7. E.g. B.M. Metzger, who claims that most scholars 'are still inclined to regard the Alexandrian text as on the whole the best ancient recension and the one most nearly approximating the original', *The Text of the New Testament* (OUP, 1968), p. 216.

8. For its influence on the *New English Bible*, see F.W. Danker in *The New English Bible Reviewed*, ed. D.E. Nineham (Epworth, 1965), p. 51; and on the United Bible Societies' Edition of 1966, see J.K. Elliott's 'Can We Recover the Original New Testament?', *Theology* 77 (1974), pp. 344-45.

9. Correspondence in April, September, and October, 1853 in the unpublished letters of Hort, *The Theological Correspondence of F.J.A. Hort* in the Cambridge University Library (CUL Add. MS 6597).

10. CUL *op.cit.* By 'numbering' is meant the practice of weighing manuscript evidence purely by numerical support for a reading.

11. *Lightfoot Correspondence*, Chapter Library, Durham. The references are to passages where Westcott and Hort had diverged sharply from the *Authorised Version*.

12. *Life and Letters of B.F. Westcott*, I (Macmillan, 1903), p. 399.

13. *Op. cit.*, p. 281.

14. CUL *op. cit.*, August 3rd 1862.

15. *Op. cit.*, June, July 1869.

16. *Op. cit.*, letter no. 168 (undated).

17. *Life and Letters of B.F. Westcott*, I, p. 400.

18. CUL *op. cit.*, October 9th 1865.

19. CUL *op. cit.*, January 1865.

20. Owen Chadwick, *The Victorian Church*, II, p. 44.

21. CUL *op. cit.*, July 7th 1870.

22. CUL Add. MS 6941.

23. Bodleian MS Eng. misc. δ 140, *Sanday Correspondence*, August 2nd 1889. Westcott, Lightfoot, W.F. Moulton and W. Milligan are among those Hort mentions as being allies.

24. Chadwick, *The Victorian Church*, II, p. 49.

25. CUL Add. MS 6597; January 1882.

26. The articles were later published as *The Revision Revised* (John Murray, 1883).

27. CUL *op.cit.*, February 1881.

28. *Op.cit.*, November 14th 1881.

29. *William F. Moulton*, W. Fiddian Moulton (Isbister, 1899), pp. 100-101.

30. O. Chadwick, *The Victorian Church*, II, pp. 53-55.

31. *William F. Moulton*, p. 209. Seven minute books are to be found in Cambridge University Library (CUL Add. MSS 6920-7).

32. E.g. by David L. Edwards, *Leaders of the Church of England 1828-1944*, p. 185.

33. LL II p. 366. The letter was, in fact, never sent.

Notes to Chapter 7

1. LL II pp. 368-69 (the words of Armitage Robinson, one of Hort's students).

2. *Contemporary Review* (July 1889), p. 47. The article is discussed in more detail in Chapter 8.

3. Henry Ryle, *Cambridge Review* (8th December 1892).

4. A return for 1886 shows 11 and 9 people respectively attending his two courses, compared with 300-350 and 30-60 for two of Westcott's (quoted in Chadwick, *The Victorian Church*, II, p. 453).

5. 'The Late Professor Hort', J.A. Robinson, *The Expositor* VII, 4th Series (1893), p. 70.

6. J.A. Robinson, *op. cit.*, p. 69.

7. 'On the Brethren' and 'St. Paul and the Three'.

8. *The Development of English Theology in the Nineteenth Century* (Longmans Green, 1913), p. 232.

9. See, for example, W. Bauer, *Orthodoxy and Heresy in Earliest Christianity* (SCM, 1972), and R.N. Longenecker, *The Christology of Early Jewish Christianity* (SCM, 1970).

10. H.E. Ryle in *Dictionary of National Biography*, Suppl. Vol. II (Smith, Elder & Co., 1901), p. 446.

11. The original intention was to continue beyond the Apostolic age, but this hope was not fulfilled.

12. 'Dr. Hort's Life and Works', *Journal of Theological Studies* I (1900), p. 386. Strong felt the whole book was 'minimising' and argued that Hort's scientific temper of mind unsuited him for historical enquiry.

13. *The Church and the Ministry* (Longmans, 1886), p. 195.

14. *The Reconstruction of Belief* (John Murray, 1926), p. 757.

15. In *Essays on the Early History of the Church and Ministry*, ed. H.B. Swete (Macmillan, 1918), p. 41.

16. 'Discussion of the Ministry in late Nineteenth-Century Anglicanism', *The Church Quarterly* July (1969), p. 60. Among the other studies was Lightfoot's famous dissertation on 'The Christian Ministry' in his commentary on Philippians.

17. *Essays Congregational and Catholic*, quoted by R.N. Flew, *Jesus and His Church* (Epworth, 1943), p. 10.

18. In his essay 'The Christian Ministry', *St. Paul's Epistle to the Philippians* (see especially p. 268).

19. E.g. LL II p. 59.

20. In 1897 Sanday described it as the fullest and the best vindication of Pauline authorship that had been made in English, and claimed that it marked a turning-point in critical controversy over the letter; *The American Journal of Theology* 1 (1897), p. 113.

21. CE pp. 265-94, CS pp. 71-82, 199-209.

22. W. Sanday, *Inspiration* (Longmans Green, 1894), pp. 129f.

23. LL II p. 294. Robertson Smith had met much opposition to his views in Scotland, and had been forced to resign from his Professorship in the Free Church College in Aberdeen.

24. LL II p. 312: 'As far as I can judge without that thorough independent investigation of the whole subject-matter which alone would entitle me to speak with full confidence, it seems likely enough that. . . Colenso's writings will be ultimately found to contain some materials of permanent value in the midst of much that will not bear investigation'.

25. 'The Study of the New Testament', *Journal of Theological Studies* 42 (1941), pp. 5-6.

26. *A Memoir of Herbert Edward Ryle*, Maurice H. Fitzgerald (Macmillan, 1928), p. 78.

27. *Op. cit.*, pp. 54, 92, 94.

28. See LL I p. 187, LL II pp. 29, 65, 281 for comments on these.

29. LL I pp. 434-35, LL II p. 278.

30. See CS pp. 58-59, WTL p. 49.

31. *The Interpretation of the New Testament 1861-1961*, p. 96.

32. E.g. L.E. Elliott-Binns, *English Thought 1860-1960: The Theological Aspect* (Longmans Green, 1956), p. 160; J.K. Mozley, *Some Tendencies in British Theology* (SPCK, 1951), p. 15.

33. Quoted in J.C. Hawkins, *Horae Synopticae* (OUP, 1909), p. v.

Notes to Chapter 8

1. *Dictionary of National Biography*, Vol. 33, pp. 232-40.

2. *Contemporary Review* (July 1889), p. 47.

3. See above pp. 87f.

4. See above p. 83.

5. CUL Add. MS 6597; January 30th 1858.
6. See O. Chadwick, *The Victorian Church*, II, p. 73.
7. Cf. a remark by Lord Acton on Döllinger, the Roman Catholic scholar: 'He knew too much to write. . . he would not write with imperfect materials and to him the materials were always imperfect', quoted in G. Himmelfarb, *Victorian Minds* (Weidenfeld, 1968), p. 173.
8. He took a whole Easter holiday in Italy to decide (LL II pp. 371-72).
9. Hort could not, however, support the programmes of pressure groups like the Church Reform Association, since he believed that reform must come from within the church and not be imposed from without.

Notes to Epilogue

1. Alan G.M. Stephenson, *The Rise and Decline of English Modernism* (SPCK, 1984), p. 44.
2. The Cambridge University undergraduate theological society is called 'The Hort Society'.

BIBLIOGRAPHY

A. *Primary Works*

1. *Letters*
a. *Unpublished*
Bodleian Library, Oxford: Correspondence of Mark Pattison (MSS Pattison 52, 54).
—Sanday Correspondence (MSS Eng. misc. 123 (ii) 140).
Cambridge University Library: Selections from the Theological Correspondence of
    F.J.A. Hort (Add. MS 6597).
—New Testament Letters I (Add. MS 6946).
Chapter Library, Durham: The Lightfoot Correspondence and Papers.

b. *Published Life and Letters of Fenton John Anthony Hort* by Arthur Hort (2 vols.;
    Macmillan, 1896).

2. *Books* (In every case the publisher is Macmillan.)
Two Dissertations (1876).
The New Testament in the Original Greek. Vol. I Test. Vol. II Intrroduction and Appendix
    (with B.F. Westcott; 1881).
The Way the Truth the Life (1893; 2nd edn, 1894).
Judaistic Christianity (1894).
Prolegomena to St. Paul's Epistles to the Romans and the Ephesians (1895).
The Ante Nicene Fathers (1895).
The Christian Ecclesia (1897).
Village Sermons (1897).
Cambridge and Other Sermons (1898).
The First Epistle of St. Peter I^1-II^{17} (1898).
Village Sermons in Outline (1900).
The Clementine Recognitions (1901).
Clement of Alexandria: Stromateis, Book 7 (Introduction and Notes, with J.B. Mayor;
    1902).
The Apocalypse of St. John I-III (1908).
The Epistle of St. James I^1-IV^7 (1909).

3. *Essays, articles, etc.*
Essay on S.T. Coleridge (*Cambridge Essays*, CUP, 1856).
Article on J.B. Lightfoot (*Dictionary of National Biography*, Vol. 33; Smith, Elder &
    Co., 1893). A full list of Hort's published essays and articles is included in LL II
    pp. 492-95.

4. *Miscellaneous*
Cambridge University Library: Notes on the Revision of the English Bible (Add. MS
    6950).
—New Testament Revision Company Register of Attendance (Add. MS 6941).
—Minute Books of New Testament Revision and Revision of Apocrypha (Add. MSS
    6935-40, 6920-27).

B. *Secondary Works*

1. *Books*

(This list includes only books referred to in the notes.)

Abbott E. and Campbell L., *The Life and Letters of Benjamin Jowett* (John Murray, 1897).

Anderson H. and Barclay W., ed., *The New Testament in Historical and Contemporary Perspective* (OUP, 1965).

Bauer, W. *Orthodoxy and Heresy in Earliest Christianity* (SCM, 1972).

Beare, F.W. *The First Epistle of Peter* (Blackwell, 1958).

Burgon, J.W. *The Revision Revised* (John Murray, 1883).

Chadwick, O. *The Victorian Church*, 2 vols. (Black, 1966, 1970).

Clark, A.C. *The Primitive Text of the Gospels and Acts* (OUP, 1914).

Cuming, G.T. ed., *Studies in Church History*, Vol. III (Brill, 1966).

Dale, A.W.W. *The Life of R.W. Dale of Birmingham* (Hodder and Stoughton, 1898).

Edwards, D.L. *Leaders of the Church of England* 1828-1944 (OUP, 1971).

Elliott-Binns, L.E. *English Thought 1860-1900: The Theological Aspect* (Longmans Green, 1956).

Ellis, I. *Seven Against Christ: A Study of 'Essays and Reviews'* (Brill, 1980).

Essays and Reviews (4th edn; Longmans Green, 1861).

Fitzgerald, M.H. *A Memoir of Herbert Edward Ryle* (Macmillan, 1928).

Flew, R.N. *Jesus and His Church* (2nd edn; Epworth, 1943).

Foakes Jackson, F.J. and Lake K. eds., *The Beginnings of Christianity, III: The Text of Acts* (Macmillan, 1926).

Gore, C. *The Church and the Ministry* (Longmans, 1886).

Gore, C. *The Reconstruction of Belief* (John Murray, 1926).

Hawkins, J.C. *Horae Synopticae* (OUP, 1899; 2nd edn, 1909).

Himmelfarb, G. *Victorian Minds* (Weidenfeld, 1968).

Howard, W.F. *The Romance of New Testament Scholarship* (Epworth, 1949).

Lightfoot, J.B. *Saint Paul's Epistle to the Philippians* (Macmillan, 1868; 1898 edn).

Longenecker, R.N. *The Christology of Early Jewish Christianity* (SCM, 1970).

Louth, A. *Discerning the Mystery* (Clarendon, 1983).

Major H.D.A. and Cross, F.L. ed., *Principles and Precepts* (Blackwell, 1927).

Maurice, F. ed., *The Life of Frederick Denison Maurice*, 2 vols. (Macmillan, 1884).

Metzger, B. *The Text of the New Testament* (OUP, 1968).

Moulton, W. Fiddian *William F. Moulton: A Memoir* (Isbister, 1899).

Mozley, J.K. *Some Tendencies in British Theology from the Publication of 'Lux Mundi' to the Present Day* (SPCK, 1951).

Neill, S. *The Interpretation of the New Testament 1861-1961* (OUP, 1966).

Nineham, D.E. ed., *The New English Bible Reviewed* (Epworth, 1965).

Pusey, E.B. Tracts 67-70: *Scriptural Views of Holy Baptism* (3rd edn; Rivingtons, 1840).

Ramsey, A.M. *F.D. Maurice and the Conflicts of Modern Theology* (CUP, 1951).

Robinson, J.A.T. *Joseph Barber Lightfoot* (Dean and Chapter of Durham, 1981).

Rowell, G. *Hell and the Victorians* (Clarendon, 1974).

Rupp, E.G. *Hort and the Cambridge Tradition* (CUP, 1968).

Sanday, W.M. *Inspiration* (Longmans Green, 1894).

Stephenson, A.G.M. *The Rise and Decline of English Modernism* (SPCK, 1984).

Storr, V.F. *The Development of English Theology in the Nineteenth Century, 1800-60* (Longmans Green, 1913).

Streeter, B.H. *The Four Gospels* (Macmillan, 1924).

Swete, H.B. ed., *Essays on the Early History of the Church and Ministry* (Macmillan, 1918).
Symondson, A. ed., *The Victorian Crisis of Faith* (SPCK, 1970).
Tulloch, J. *Movements of Religious Thought in Britain During the Nineteenth Century* (Longmans Green, 1885).
Vidler, A. *F.D. Maurice and Company* (SCM, 1966).
Westcott, A.F. *Life and Letters of Brooke Foss Westcott*, 2 vols. (Macmillan, 1903).

2. *Articles*
(The following articles have been especially helpful; others are referred to in the text).
Creed, J.M. 'The Study of the New Testament', *Journal of Theological Studies* 42 (1941).
Hort, A.F. 'Fenton John Anthony Hort', *Modern Churchman* 17 (1927).
Mayor J.B. and Murray, J.O.F. 'Obituary' and 'Memoir and list of works published and unpublished', *Classical Review* 7 (1893).
Robertson, A. 'Hort on I Peter', *Journal of Theological Studies* 1 (1900).
Robinson, J.A. 'Dr Hort on the Apocalypse', *Journal of Theological Studies* 10 (1908).
Robinson, J.A. and Ramsay, W.M. 'The Late Professor Hort', *The Expositor* VII, 4th Series (1893).
Ryle, H.E. 'F.J.A. Hort', *Dictionary of National Biography*, Supplement Vol. II (Smith, Elder & Co., 1901).
Sanday, W.M. 'The Future of English Theology', *Contemporary Review* (July 1889).
Sanday, W.M. 'The Life and Letters of F.J.A. Hort', *American Journal of Theology* 1 (1897).
Stone, D. 'Hort's Hulsean Lectures on the Way the Truth the Life', *Church Quarterly Review* 38 (1894).
Strong, T.B. 'Dr Hort's Life and Works', *Journal of Theological Studies* 1 (1900).

3. *Other Works*
Bubb, I.M. The Theology of F.J.A. Hort in Relation to Nineteenth Century Thought (1956, unpublished PhD thesis, Manchester University Library).

INDEX

INDEX OF AUTHORS CITED